Making Great
SAUSAGE
AT HOME

D1298038

LARK BOOKS

A Division of Sterling Publishing Co., Inc
New York

Making Great
SAUSAGE
AT HOME

30 SAVORY LINKS
FROM AROUND THE WORLD

PLUS DOZENS
OF DELICIOUS
SAUSAGE DISHES

**Chris
Kobler**

JANE LAFERLA
Editor

CHRIS BRYANT
Book and cover design
and production, food styling,
and photostyling

EVAN BRACKEN
Photography

HEATHER SMITH
Editorial assistance

HANNES CHAREN
Production assistance

VAL ANDERSON
Proofreader

Library of Congress Cataloging-in-Publication Data

Kobler, Chris, 1946–
    Making great sausage at home: 30 savory links from around the world
plus dozens of delicious sausage dishes / by Chris Kobler.—1st ed.
      p. cm.
    Includes bibliographical references and index.
    ISBN 1-57990-131-X (hardcover) ISBN 1-57990-325-8 (paperback)
    1. Cookery (Sausages) 2. Sausages. I. Title
TX749.5.S28K63   1999
641.6'6—dc21   99-25466
                                          CIP

641.66 Kobl (handwritten)

10 9 8 7 6 5 4 3 2 1

Published by Lark Books, a division of
Sterling Publishing Co., Inc.
387 Park Avenue South, New York, N.Y. 10016

© 1999, Chris Kobler

Distributed in Canada by Sterling Publishing,
c/o Canadian Manda Group, One Atlantic Ave., Suite 105
Toronto, Ontario, Canada M6K 3E7

Distributed in the U.K. by:
Guild of Master Craftsman Publications Ltd.
Castle Place, 166 High Street, Lewes East Sussex, England BN7 1XU
Tel: (+ 44) 1273 477374, Fax: (+ 44) 1273 478606,
Email: pubs@thegmcgroup.com, Web: www.gmcpublications.com

Distributed in Australia by Capricorn Link (Australia) Pty Ltd., P.O. Box 704,
Windsor, NSW 2756 Australia

If you have questions or comments about this book, please contact:
Lark Books
67 Broadway
Asheville, NC 28801
(828) 236-9730

Printed in China

ISBN 1-57990-131-X (hardcover) ISBN 1-57990-325-8 (paperback)

acknowledgements

I happily dedicate this book to my daughters, Nora and Emily.

I WISH TO THANK the staff of Lark Books for the vote of confidence in allowing me to write this book. To owner, dance partner, and Capo di tutti Capo, Rob Pulleyn; publisher Carol Taylor; senior editor (and friend) Deborah Morgenthal; editor Jane LaFerla; art director Chris Bryant; and photographer Evan Bracken. Actually, they've all become friends. My tasters-in- waiting (including all of the above) earned my thanks and a guest pass to the gymnasium— you know who you are. I cooked it and you all came. Hand holders and encouragers include Brigid, Bob, Doug and Angela, Pam and Paul, Hank and Marita, and the gang at Gold Hill. Special thanks to Victor Giancola. Thanks also to the Vienna Sausage Company, Neto Sausage Company, Panizzera Meat Company, The National Hot Dog and Sausage Council, the Sheboygan, Wisconsin, Chamber of Commerce and their Bratwurst Days celebration and the New Braunfels, Texas, Chamber of Commerce, and their Best of the Wurst festival.

preface

"ONE CANNOT THINK WELL, LOVE WELL, SLEEP WELL, IF ONE HAS NOT
DINED WELL."—Virginia Woolf

SOMEWHERE, in an all-but-forgotten text, I once read that, when what you
are doing is what you are, what you are doing is art. I believe that feeding
people can be fine art, ephemeral perhaps, but art nonetheless. I have found
that I express myself best in this lovely melding of nurture and craft.

"EATING IS NOT MERELY A MATERIAL PLEASURE. EATING WELL GIVES
A SPECTACULAR JOY TO LIFE AND CONTRIBUTES IMMENSELY TO
GOODWILL AND HAPPY COMPANIONSHIP. IT IS OF GREAT IMPORTANCE
TO THE MORALE."— Elsa Schiaparelli

THAT SAID, I need also tell you that nothing pleases me quite so much as to
find myself well regarded by my fellows. My way of sticking to the ribs of
your regard is to feed you meals that you will remember. To correct a supersti-
tion of the food-frightened who believe food is merely a substitute for love, I
believe that feeding is loving. Thus in feeding you, I offer you intimacy by
providing your most basic need—and I wish to do so beautifully.

"AFTER A GOOD DINNER ONE CAN FORGIVE ANYBODY, EVEN ONE'S OWN
RELATIONS."—Oscar Wilde

WE CAN, all of us, produce in our own homes all but the most pyrotechnic
of dishes. I have discovered in a lifetime of feeding people that wonderful food can be produced by virtually anyone, anywhere, anytime, with easily
found ingredients and common tools. I have been able to create wonderful
unplanned dinner parties when trapped in dormitories, stranded in beach
houses, exiled on camping trips, jungles, deserts, and islands. No matter the
locale, we (whoever it was that made the other portion of we) were able to
delight ourselves with delicious improvised meals that were precisely rendered.

"ONE HALF OF THE WORLD CANNOT UNDERSTAND THE PLEASURES OF
THE OTHER."—Jane Austen, *Emma*, ch. 9 (1816).

IT IS TRUE that there are people who are food blind (bless their hearts); those
unable, or unwilling, to open themselves to new combinations of flavor and
texture. There are also finicky eaters, food fanatics, and food police constantly
on the prowl for violations against their personal food codes. There are many
who claim they are unable to cook. While all of the above may be unlikely to
read this book, they are all welcome at my table.

contents

introduction

Myron Floren (left), longtime Lawrence Welk band member, celebrates with friends at The Best of The Wurst Festival held annually in New Braunfels, Texas. Photograph courtesy of the New Braunfels Chamber of Commerce

During Sheboyagn, Wisconsin's Bratwurst Day, cooks turn a large rack of bratwurst that will feed revelers at this annual celebration. Photograph courtesy of the Sheboygan County Chamber of Commerce

sausages are a celebration!

IF YOU DOUBT THIS SIMPLE ACCOLADE, ALLOW YOUR SENSE MEMORY TO ROAM. Picture an Italian street festival. (Little Italy in New York or the North End of Boston immediately come to mind.) Smell the miles of Italian sausage sizzling on the grills in the booths that line the streets. A vendor beckons, places a done-to-perfection beauty in a sliced length of crusty bread, then tops the whole thing off with a blanket of peppers cooked in olive oil.

Conjure up the remembrance of the best hot dog you've ever eaten. Was it at a ball park—a house special smothered in relish and mustard, and washed down with a cold beer and a winning home run? Was it at the beach—a natural accompaniment to sunburn, salt air, and a leisurely stroll on the boardwalk? Or was it the first one you impaled on a stick and roasted over a smoky campfire—which rendered it slightly charred but still delicious beyond belief?

Whether it's bratwurst cooked outside and shared on a steamy summer night with friends and neighbors, Polish sausage so juicy and luscious that you could almost hear the skin crack at first bite, or a simple salami sandwich on white in your lunch box, the remembrances of sausages past are as personal and numerous as the varied experiences of life. But you'll soon find that it's the pleasure of sausage present and future that await you when you learn to make your own.

Today's savvy cooks are rediscovering the craft of sausage making as an important way to sample the best of the world's culinary heritage. Mention home-made sausage and inevitably someone tells how their mother or grandmother made the weekly sausage for the family, or of a cousin who still makes incredible venison sausage once a year, or that they've heard of a family who gathers together to make traditional sausage as a part of their holiday ritual. If these stories have ever inspired you to someday try making your own sausage, now is the time.

A HISTORY

Sausages can be considered an almost perfect food. They combine wonderful herbs and spices, flavorful meats, vegetables, and grains in a natural casing. They can be poached, boiled, steamed, baked, roasted, or grilled. In their charmingly odd package, the ingredients meld when cooked, basted in their own savory juices. Then, when eaten, the contained goodness bursts upon your palate in the most festive way possible. Is it any wonder that many cultures through the centuries have created innumerable local festivals to celebrate, honor, and consume this incredible food?

Sausages have been with us for a very long time. The word comes from Latin, *salsicius*, meaning prepared by salting, which is a simple method of preserving meats. Sausage making is one of the oldest methods of food preparation. Virtually every culture has developed sausage to preserve meats that could not all be consumed at the time of slaughter. What began as safe and economical food storage, over time became cuisine.

The earliest mention of sausage was in the *Odyssey* by Homer in the 9th century B.C. People in this era and earlier knew that without preservation, meats would rapidly become unfit for consumption. They learned to cut or grind meat into small pieces, season it with salt and spices, and then to dry it.

The sausage was paid early tribute by the Greek playwright Epicharmus, who wrote Orya (The Sausage) in about 500 B.C. Sausages have been favored by plain folk and royalty alike over the centuries; Nebuchadnezzar, the Babylonian king, may have been the first royal fan of this food.

The preservation process used by ancient cultures, including Chinese, Greek, Roman, and Babylonian, produced meat that was essentially fermented and dried. You can only wonder how many

Panizzera Meat Company of Occidental, California, was founded in 1914 by Constante and Margaret (photo left), Italian immigrants from the Lake Como region. Today their grandson, Bob Panizzera, uses the family recipes to carry on the company's famous sausage making traditions. Photographs courtesy of Panizzera Meat Company

Since 1948 The Neto Sausage Company of Santa Clara, California, has been producing linguiça, a Portuguese sausage, from a generations-old family recipe. They also produce andouille, chorizo, and Spanish longaniza. Photographs courtesy of Neto Sausage Company

people perished in the attempt to achieve safety? The larger dried sausages that we are familiar with today, such as salami, probably most closely resemble these earliest sausages.

A favorite recipe of butchers in Ancient Rome included cutting pork and beef into small pieces, adding salt, pine nuts, cumin seed, bay leaves, and black pepper. They would stuff the mixture into animal skins and hang them to dry in special rooms. They knew the meat was safe to consume many months later. These Roman sausage makers formed guilds and guarded their secrets closely. Furthermore, if you believe that we are overinspected and regulated today, Roman shops were inspected and licensed by their government.

Sausage has a political history as well. In 320 A.D., the Roman Emperor Constantine the Great banned certain pagan festivals, and, as sausage was a featured food at the festivals, he banned those also! Sausage production at that time never quite dried up, it merely went underground until the ban was later repealed in response to popular opinion.

Through the ages sausage has become a universal food; it is easily recognizable throughout the world as sausage no matter what the locals call it. The unique and interesting combinations of the different flavors from each culture provide for almost endless varia-tion to this simple food—and perhaps that is sausage's enduring charm.

Even when family sausage recipes have crossed the oceans and taken up residence in other lands, sausage continues to ignite fierce loyalties. Be it British bangers, Cajun boudin, andouille and chau-rice, French saucisson a l'ail, Chinese sweet sausage, Swedish potato sausage, Italian fennel sausage and salami, Mexican chorizo, Portuguese linguiça, Pennsylvania Dutch scrapple, Southern liver mush, Scottish black pudding, bratwurst, braunschweiger, wienerwurst, bologna, genoa, cotto, mortadella, cottechino, or kielbasa, everyone seems to have a favorite sausage inspired by the traditions of a national or cultural cuisine.

GETTING STARTED

Now on to the meat of the matter (or, the matter of the meat). Let me confess that I came to this project uninformed but eager and curious. That is to say, I was recruited to write this book not because I was known as a great charcuterier but because I am a writer who likes to cook. So I researched and stuffed, cooked and served, and I received immediate accolades.

To judge response to the recipes featured in this book, I prepared many sausage-centered meals and hosted sausage tastings for family and friends. While my guests thought the sausages wonderful, they seemed more impressed by the fact that they were homemade. Many people regard some cooking as beyond the home pale, considering it either too technical or difficult. With this attitude, they automatically exclude, to their own detriment, great recipes from their menus as being beyond their range of culinary skills.

In fact, I have found sausage making to be both easy and fun. Since it requires very little equipment, it is also economical. In addition, when you make your own sausage, you know exactly what's in it, and can be assured that the ingredients are as fresh as possible. I would even recommend to you to gather a group of friends for an evening of fun, frivolity, and sausage making. For now, forget fondue, pack away the pasta machine, and bring out the grinder. Aside from the lighthearted companionship of a unique shared cooking experience, you will be producing a product that is indisputably delicious.

Two young immigrants from Austria-Hungary started the Vienna Sausage Company in 1893 when they first sold their sausage at the Chicago Columbia Exposition. While known for their exceptional hot dogs, Vienna Sausage of Chicago, Illinois, also produces bratwurst, polish sausage, and a variety of deli meats and products. Photographs courtesy of the Vienna Sausage Company

During the 1950s, movie actress Jayne Mansfield reigned for one year as the National Hot Dog Queen. She is seen here dispensing her duties.
Photograph courtesy of the National Hot Dog and Sausage Council

HOW TO USE THIS BOOK

The basics section will take you through the rudiments of sausage making. You will learn about the equipment you need and how to use it, as well as ingredients, fat ratios, and the different sausage casings. Pay special attention to the section on sanitation for the proper handling and storage of meat.

The first recipe will be for a bulk breakfast sausage. Try it to get a general feel for sausage making, and then prepare it as a wonderful part of a country breakfast accompanied by fresh biscuits and gravy. You'll find a section with sausage recipes grouped according to their countries or cultures of origin. The last section of the book features recipes from around the world that use sausage as the main ingredient, plus extra recipes for complements to your sausage such as mustard, spreads, and relishes.

If squeamish feelings about handling the ingredients have held you back from attempting this craft, I encourage you to set aside your preconceived notions and to try one recipe. Once you do, you won't think twice about the ingredients or the process as being much different from other from-scratch cooking projects. Besides, you'll find homemade sausage so superior to store-bought, that the process will ultimately become an enjoyable means of procuring the product.

It's also my hope (and duty to inform you as an adventurous, inquisitive cook), that once you feel comfortable with the process of sausage making, you will experiment with your own recipes. That secret ingredient you stumble upon may be the beginning of a guarded family recipe.

So, lets get started—and remember to smile—since sausages are the ultimate cartoon food. The hot dog squirts out of the bun. The dog runs out of the butcher shop with a string of brats waving in the breeze. Somewhere, not far from where you're sitting, some joker is driving down a highway in a car built and painted to look like a wiener. And I say that there is much more fun to be had.

first steps of making sausage

sau·sage (sô′sĭj), *n.* finely chopped and seasoned meat, especially pork, usually stuffed into a prepared animal intestine or other casing, and cooked or cured.

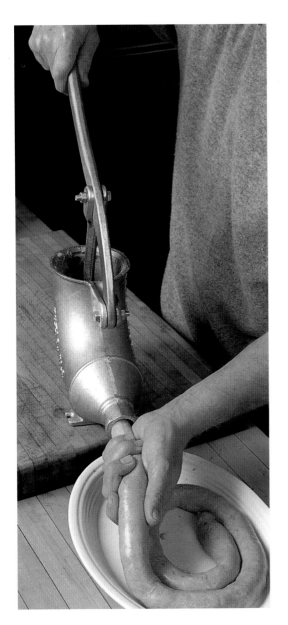

...SO SAYS THE DICTIONARY. Of course there are no limitations to ingredients and styles. In *The Great Book of Sausages*, by Antony and Araminta Hippesley Coxe, the undisputed encyclopedia of this cuisine, 600 types of sausage are listed and described from Armadillo sausage to Zwyczajna. (I hope you can surmise by the spelling of the last sausage that it is of Polish origin.) As you study the topic further, you'll find that the principle ingredient of any one sausage recipe may not even be meat—the spectrum ranges from blood to tofu, and can even include beans and fruit. I know of recipes for chocolate salami.

While sausage casing comes traditionally from the intestines of pigs, sheep, or cows, any spare animal part or edible material may be recruited to serve the simple function of holding the filling together in a neat package. Some alternative animal-based casings can include a boned pig's foot, chicken necks, sheep's stomachs, beef bladders, and caul fat (the fat on the membrane that extends from the stomach to the large intestine).

A common commercial casing is made from collagen, the protein found in connective tissue, which is derived entirely from animal products, then processed and formed into a continuous hollow tube. If you buy Polish or smoked sausage at the grocery store, it is most likely stuffed in collagen casings. Artificial casings are made from cellulose and plastic. Technically you could use hollowed-out vegetables and edible leaves as casings.

Of course the sausage need not be stuffed. Fresh, bulk sausage is chopped meat mixed together with herbs, spices, and flavorings, and often some form of binder or extender, such as egg or bread crumbs, which helps hold the seasoned meat together for cooking. You can make the breakfast sausage below using only a mixing bowl and a frying pan. Once you make this recipe, you will know the essential procedure that universally extends through all the recipes about seasoning and mixing the meat.

BULK BREAKFAST SAUSAGE

INGREDIENTS

½ lb (224 g) ground pork

½ lb (224 g) ground lamb

1 egg

½ cup (70 g) seasoned bread crumbs

½ teaspoon rubbed sage

½ teaspoon salt

Black pepper and red pepper flakes to taste

½ cup (120 mL) milk

1 tablespoon all-purpose flour

METHOD

Thoroughly clean a large mixing bowl in soapy water and rinse, then scald the bowl with boiling water. (I prefer stainless steel bowls, but ceramic or heavy plastic will do.) Your only other tool will be your hands—so wash and rinse them well. Put all the ingredients, except for the milk and flour, into the bowl. Using your hands, reach across the ingredients, grasp a handful, and push it down through the center of the mass. Turn the bowl a quarter turn and repeat. Continue turning and pushing down until well mixed.

Refrigerate the mixture for 1 hour to allow the flavors to meld and strengthen. Remove from the refrigerator and form the mixture into balls, then flatten into patties, each approximately 2 to 3 inches (5 to 7.5 cm) across. In the frying pan, brown the patties over medium-high heat, then lower the temperature to medium and cook through. You want the juices of

the patties to run clear without a trace of pink. When the patties are cooked, keep them warm before serving by placing the sausages on a heated platter in a warm oven.

To make the gravy, pour off all but 1 to 2 tablespoons of fat. With the pan at a medium temperature, gradually sprinkle the flour into the pan and cook to remove the flour taste, stirring and scraping to get all of the browned bits into the gravy. After about 3 minutes, gradually pour in the milk, stirring all the while. Continue until the gravy thickens, approximately 4 to 5 minutes.

Serve the sausages with a side dish of prepared eggs, and pour the gravy over hot, fresh biscuits. (You'll find another recipe for bulk breakfast sausage on page 93.)

MAKING A COUNTRY BREAKFAST

1. Form the patties.

2. Fry them until well browned on both sides, then drain them on a paper towel.

3. Make the gravy by first browning the flour in the hot grease.

4. Add the milk and blend into the flour until thickened.

5. To make the eggs, pour the beaten eggs into a clean pan.

6. Season eggs with salt and pepper.

TYPES OF SAUSAGE

Fresh Sausage

The preceding recipe for breakfast sausage is an example of fresh, bulk sausage made of minced raw meat and spices. Fresh sausage, made this way, is formed and fried or grilled soon after it is made, just as you would a hamburger, or the uncooked mixture is frozen for future use. Fresh sausage may be broken up and cooked before using it as an ingredient in other dishes such as casseroles or sauces. Bulk sausage left raw should be wrapped and can be refrigerated for three days or frozen for three months.

Fresh sausage is also the *forcemeat*, defined as chopped up, seasoned meat or fish, that you stuff into casings. Once encased, fresh sausage may be fried, grilled, poached, baked, or simmered. The recipes in this book focus on fresh sausage that is to be prepared and eaten soon after you make it or frozen for future use.

Smoked Sausage

Sausages can be either cold- or hot-smoked. I find the flavor that results (particularly with aromatic woods such as hickory, mesquite, and apple woods) from smoking is delicious. Since you are smoking the sausages to both impart flavor and to retard spoilage, it is important that you follow the instructions on your smoker when you are trying this "old fashioned" method.

Cold-smoked sausages are smoked over a low heat for a long time. Depending on the recipe, this can mean many hours or even days. Cold smoking dries the sausages somewhat but does not fully cook them, so that any cold-smoked meats must be cooked before eating. They are, however, dried enough to extend their refrigerated life beyond that of fresh sausage, and can be kept, wrapped and refrigerated, for up to two weeks.

Hot-smoked sausages (such as bologna and mortadella) are smoked over a higher heat. The heat makes them ready to eat and they need no further cooking. Like cold-smoked sausages, hot-smoked sausages may be refrigerated for up to two weeks. You may freeze both cold- and hot-smoked sausages, and can keep them in the freezer for up to six months. For more information about hot-smoking see page 000.

You can approximate the smoky flavor (rather well, actually) by using liquid smoke, a bottled flavoring made from condensed smoke. A very small amount, approximately ¼ teaspoon per pound of meat, is effective. Remember, of course, that this meat is only flavored, not treated, and is still raw, so you will need to prepare it just as you would fresh meat.

Cured Sausage

Cured sausage (such as salami and pepperoni) is firmer and keeps much longer than fresh or smoked sausage. Curing meats retards spoilage by removing most of the moisture. In order to keep the meat from spoiling as it dries, it is necessary to treat the meat with small amounts of chemical curing agents.

There are two basic substances used in curing meats, *nitrates* and *nitrites*. The use of these agents has become controversial, with claims that these substances may be carcinogenic. I can recommend *Great Sausage Recipes and Meat Curing*, by Rytek Kutas for a thorough discussion of the process, and an argument for its safety.

Whatever your belief about the various additives used in curing meats, there is one issue that every layperson can agree on; the diseases that can result from uncured or improperly cured meat are well known and severe. Like many of the substances we all consume in one form or another, the additives used for curing meats can be toxic to some of us in any amount and to all of us in large amounts. I will allow that I occasionally eat commercially cured meats, such as bacon, Genoa salami, and cured Kielbasa, believing that moderation is the key to enjoyment.

To conclude this discussion, I am neither a chemist nor a physician, and my approach is to eschew home curing of meats. My concern is that I have no way of knowing (at least in advance of consuming the product) if I have used the correct amount of chemicals to protect me and my guests from both the disease and the cure (pun intended). For the purposes of this book, I do not offer recipes for home curing sausage. Each of the recipes may be smoked if you like and, as I indicated earlier, for safety's sake, always refer to your smoker's operating manual for temperatures, smoking times, and the kinds of wood to use.

CASINGS

There is no delicate way to introduce this topic. Simply stated, many sausages are encased, and the casings are, more often than not, of animal origin. If you are a true sausage lover, this should not faze you in the least. You must admit, natural casings are the ultimate example of waste-not-want-not, recycling, and using what you have at hand. If you have any misgivings, perhaps the follow-ing information will demystify the concept, and you can view casings as just one more efficiently convenient natural ingredient used in the world's cuisine.

Up until the 20th century, all sausages were stuffed in natural casings made primarily from animal intestines. The portion of the intestine that is used is the submucosa, a layer of connective tissue that has several properties. The submucosa is a thin and flexible tissue made of a natural protein called collagen. It is strong, almost transparent, and semi-permeable, which allows flavors such as smoke to penetrate at the same time that it protects and concentrates the flavors within. Commercially

processed natural casings do not impart conflicting flavors to the finished sausage.

Collagen, a constituent of bone, cartilage, and tendons, may be reduced by boiling to form gelatin. In this century, manufacturers have developed techniques to process collagen to make artificial edible casings of convenient sizes and shapes. Entirely artificial casings are made of plastic, cloth, and paper, and are, of course, not intended to be eaten. It stretches the point somewhat, but one could create a loose casing substitute using vegetable leaves that can enfold a forcemeat; obvious examples include grape leaves and corn husks.

Natural casings are derived from domesticated hogs, sheep, and cows. The intestines (or stomach in some cases) are stripped of fat and other membranes and thoroughly cleaned. They are often gathered together in hanks (much like yarn) and salted. Once cleaned and salted, the casings may be kept indefinitely under refrigeration.

Hog casings are easiest to work with, being quite strong and large enough to easily manipulate. Sheep casings are smaller, thinner-walled, and require delicate handling and the use of a smaller funnel when filling the casings. What are called beef middles are larger casings that come from beef but are much tougher in consistency than casings from pigs or sheep. Because hog casings are far easier to find than sheep or cow casings, all of the recipes in this book assume that you will be using hog casings.

In addition to the intestine, stomachs, bladders, and a portion of the intestine that seems equivalent to the human appendix, called the bung, are also used. These large pieces work best for bologna, salamis, liverwurst, and other large types of sausage. The best known use of the stomach is the dubious Scottish delicacy haggis (see page 56).

Of all the various types of casings, I prefer, by far, natural casings for flavor, texture, and tradition. Hog casings are inexpensive, easy to find, and versatile to use. I have been able to purchase a 60-foot (55 m) hank at a local meat-rendering plant for less than I would pay for a pound of commercially prepared sausage. Sheep casings are available through mail-order butchers and sausage suppliers. Unfortunately, it is difficult to find sheep casings in less than large commercial quantities, giving you many more casings than you would ever need for small homemade batches. If you would like to try sheep casings, perhaps you could network with other local sausage makers and split a large quantity between yourselves. Again, all of the recipes in this book assume that you will use hog casings, and I find them always acceptable.

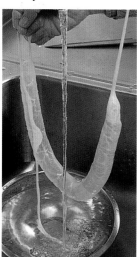

Hog casings being rinsed with water

MEAT AND FAT

One of the great advantages to making and cooking items that most people get at the store is that you have complete control over all the ingredients. It is commonplace to not want to know what goes into hot dogs. In fact, the phrase "meat and meat by-products," always gives me a chill when I read the labels. However, if you make it yourself, you will always know what goes into your recipe, and will no longer need to second-guess someone else's definition of what constitutes meat.

When you begin to make these sausages (or prepare any recipe) you might be tempted to create your own variations. This tendency is particularly strong with regard to reducing fat content. I recommend that you absolutely follow this impulse. However, you will find as have I, that low fat means dry and high fat means juicy. I will not begin to advise anyone about diet (I myself am happily ungoverned, which means I pay the price in working it off at the gym).

As you begin this culinary adventure, you might consider making the sausage with the standard amount of fat in ratio to lean which is 25 to 30 percent fat. If this traditional quantity sounds too steep for your personal fat consumption, perhaps you can compensate by eating less than traditional quantities of the finished product. As in any recipe, you can only substitute ingredients so far until it becomes a totally separate entity, rather than an authentic derivative.

That said, there are two basic approaches to the meats you will use. The first, and simplest, is to choose a cut of meat that naturally contains the approximate traditional balance of fat to lean. Boston butt pork roast, which comes from the shoulder of the pig, contains about 20 percent fat which I find almost ideal. When preparing this cut of meat, it is only necessary to remove any bone, obvious tendons, and sinew. Occasionally a roast will need more trimming or even the addition of extra fat. The best way to learn about the fat content of various cuts is to speak to your butcher.

Secondly, you can purchase a lean meat, such as tenderloin, and add minced fat in the quantities you

This well-marbled Boston butt pork roast contains approximately 20 percent fat.

wish. This is an excellent approach from the perspective of fat control, although it pushes the grocery bill to the high end, since tenderloin is one of the choicest of cuts. Furthermore, unless you wish to use a flavored fat like bacon, be sure to avoid salted fats.

When making beef, lamb, poultry, and seafood sausages, you will need to look at different requirements for preparation before grinding, including providing different fat resources. Commonly, less expensive cuts of red meats (beef and lamb) contain more connective tissue and fat throughout. For many purposes, including sausage, this is an advantage since the connective tissue produces richer flavors. The drawback is that the tougher tissues need to be laboriously cut out.

As you will see, the poultry recipes rely on available fat primarily in the form of skin. You can also collect poultry fat from roasting birds, then strain it and store it for later use. Since seafood sausages tend to have little fat, which often comes in the form of butter or oil, they need moist and brief cooking methods to help prevent them from drying out; poaching is ideal. In summary, when making sausage,

don't be too timid when talking about fat. What makes sausage such a special dish in my opinion results from packing together, within the casing, not only the meats and spices, but also the fat which becomes the cooking medium. Remember, the fat bastes and flavors the meat as the sausage cooks, bathing it with the herbs and spices that infuse the taste.

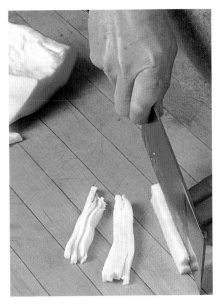

Adding additional fat may be necessary when making sausage with leaner cuts of meat.

sausage
making
basics

Following are the basic concepts and techniques for home sausage making:

EQUIPMENT

PREPARATION

GRINDING, EMULSIFYING, AND HAND CUTTING

MIXING

STUFFING

SANITATION

STORAGE AND COOKING

THIS CHAPTER WILL DISCUSS the equipment you will need for making sausage and introduce you to the general how-to steps. You'll find that the processes involved are very simple. Let me begin by very briefly describing the basic procedures: Grind or chop the meat; mix it with herbs, spices, and other ingredients until it becomes, by definition, forcemeat; then stuff the force-meat into a package. At this point the sausage is either cooked and eaten, or is preserved by one of several methods.

While all this sounds relatively easy, and it is for the most part, there are some skills involved in sausage making that elevate it to a craft, and I will cover these as we go along.

EQUIPMENT

Sausage making does not require a large investment in new tools. In theory, if you have a good knife, a cutting board, and a funnel, you can make sausage. However, unless you value doing things the hard way, I recommend that you add some inexpensive pieces.

Kitchen Tools

The basic, all-purpose kitchen tools listed below are ones that I assume you already have at hand. Understand that each item should be prefaced with the word "good," as in "a good, sharp knife." Good does not necessarily mean professional-grade; the tools you use should be those with which you are most comfortable and that effectively get the job done. (I'm not advocating that you run out and purchase new tools for the purposes of this book; however, if you were looking for an excuse to up grade, feel free to do so!).

Make sure the tools you use are easy to clean: A well-used plastic or wood cutting board are acceptable; chipped and pitted ones are not recommended.

BONING KNIFE optional —but you will be grateful to have one

CHEF'S KNIFE with a heavy blade, at least 8 inches (20 cm) long

CUTTING BOARDS—either wood or non-porous plastic or acrylic

FUNNEL—with a tube that you can push your thumb through (I have found that most standard funnels have spouts that are too narrow to be of use for hand stuffing sausage. The spout must be narrow enough for sliding the casing over it, and wide enough to allow the forcemeat to pass through. There are funnels made especially for making sausage; you may be lucky enough to find one—try looking in an old-fashioned hardware store.

KITCHEN SCALE—if you don't own one, buy one please! (I recommend a digital scale that is sensitive to a tenth of an ounce. There is simply no better way to portion ingredients such as meats and fats than by weight. Without a scale, it is almost impossible to guess how much meat is left after you've boned and trimmed a roast. While very experienced chefs are good at estimating weights, they still use scales.)

KITCHEN TWINE—undyed, unbleached cotton thread for tying ends and links

PARING KNIFE

PLASTIC STORAGE CONTAINERS

STAINLESS STEEL MIXING BOWLS—large enough to accommodate 4 to 5 pounds (1.8 to 2.3 kg) of meat and both of your hands

Grinders

The basic process of making the forcemeat involves either reducing the meat to a paste, or at least to small chunks. While this can be done (laboriously) with knives, effort, and patience, I recommend a grinder. You can find grinders in cookware and hardware stores.

HAND GRINDER

One of the most common and versatile grinders, or meat mincers, clamps on the edge of a worktable or kitchen counter. My grinder is imported from Poland (where sausage forms a religion), and is sold as a kit including a stuffing funnel and two round mincing plates (one coarse, one fine). To grind, you put the meat in the hopper, then turn the handle to push the ingredients via a large internal screw through the mincing plate.

You can also use the hand grinder to stuff the sausage. Once the meat is ground and the other

Hand grinder

Electric mixer with grinder attachment

Grinder attachment

ingredients mixed in to make the forcemeat, you remove the mincing plate and attach the sausage funnel. You then put the forcemeat in the hopper, and turn the handle to push it through the funnel and into the casing. I find it extremely awkward to turn the handle while manipulating the casing and much prefer using either a separate hand stuffer (see next page), or the attachment for an electric mixer.

GRINDER ATTACHMENT

The device I use most often for making sausage is the food grinder attachment for my electric mixer. Like the hand grinder, it comes with an assortment of mincer plates for grinding and a sausage funnel for stuffing. I prefer this device for three reasons: First, it is powered. Since you do not need to turn the handle to force the meat through the plates or into the funnel, both hands are free for manipulating the ingredients. Secondly, the mixer sits higher above the work surface than the hand grinder, allowing the ground extrusion or finished sausage to trail into a waiting bowl or container. And finally, of all the devices I have tried, this particular one allows the easiest and most controlled stuffing process.

Stuffing tube for grinder attachment

TO POWER OR NOT TO POWER

As with many traditional crafts, arguments can be made both ways when it comes to choosing whether to use hand- or electric- powered tools. Whatever your prefer-ence or reasons for choosing one over the other, either the hand grinder or the attachment for the electric mixer provide excellent results. Both of these devices are easy to master, disassemble easily for cleaning, can be used for both grinding and stuffing, and are almost the same price. (The attachment for the electric mixer costs a little more. However, if you don't already have an electric mixer, the cost will be substantially higher!)

Food Processor

I recommend a food processor to achieve the very fine-grained, smooth paste needed when making emulsified forcemeat, such as in hot dogs, bologna, and liver sausage. While you can continue to pass the forcemeat through the fine mincer plate on a hand grinder or grinder attachment to partially emulsify the mixture, a food processor will do the work much quicker and with much better results.

Be aware that some food authors suggest that a food processor may substitute for a grinder. I find, however, that using a food processor in this way makes it all but impossible to get an even, coarse cut when needed; some portions of the meat will become paste while others will be left too large.

Sausage stuffer

Stuffers

The most elemental sausage stuffer is your thumb and a funnel. This works extremely well and should not be discounted if you are eager to get to the recipes. You may also want to try hand stuffing to see if you like the process of making fresh sausage enough (and the delicious end product) to invest in basic equipment.

As discussed above, both a hand grinder and grinding attachment for an electric mixer include the needed components for stuffing. If you prefer using a hand grinder for making your forcemeat, I believe it's much easier to use a device designed exclusively for stuffing rather than using the grinder for stuffing. You can purchase a separate stuffer that consists of a bent tube with an arm/lever that pushes the forcemeat through a stuffing tube and into the casing. This device allows you to fill the casings with uniform pressure that you control.

Stuffing the sausage by hand

An example of everything in its place (*mise en place*), showing the ingredients for chorizo.

Cut the par-frozen meat into finger-sized pieces.

PREPARATION

Mise en place is the important culinary principle that means everything in place; it plays an important role in all cooking procedures. When you practice this principle, you will save yourself not only time and trouble, but the ultimate frustration of not having the crucial ingredient in your kitchen or the proper utensil within reach.

The most basic advice is to always read a recipe through before you begin. Determine everything you will need—and purchase enough! Individual recipes will indicate whether you need to chop vegetables, grind spices, etc., beforehand. All of this preparation should be completed by the time you begin to make the sausage.

Always be certain to follow the rules of sanitation (see page 35). Clean and dry all utensils, bowls, plastic containers, equipment, cutting boards, and work surfaces before you begin.

Preparing the Meat

Unless otherwise indicated in an individual recipe, you will need to grind the meat before mixing it with the other ingredients.In order for the meat to easily fit into the hopper of the grinder or grinder attachment, you need to first bone the meat if necessary, then cut it into manageable pieces.

Boning entails removing any obvious large bones as well as checking for and eliminating any smaller pieces of bone or bone fragments that may remain. Inspect the meat and remove as much tendon and sinew as possible. If you judge the meat to be too fatty to maintain the proper 20 to 25 percent fat to lean ratio, remove extra fat at your discretion.

I've found, and highly recommend, that boned, par-frozen (semifrozen) meat is much easier to cut. After boning, you can wrap the meat and place it in the freezer until ice crystals begin to form; or, you can thaw boned and frozen meat to the stage where you are just able to cut it easily. You want to cut the meat into finger-sized pieces. To do this, first slice the meat into slabs that are approximately 1-inch (2.5 cm) thick. Next, stack the slabs and cut them into strips. Refrigerate until ready.

Preparing the Casings

Straight from their package, casings look like wet string and feel slippery like cooked spaghetti. The recipe (and your experience) will indicate how much casing you will need. Using a knife or scissors, cut a little more than the required length. In the sink, with the water running, open one end of the casing and rinse through thoroughly several times. You may discover holes in the casing when rinsing. If you find that there are too many holes in one section, cut another length. If the portion with the leak is toward the front or back of the length, cut it off. While it isn't absolutely necessary, I like to soak the casings in fresh water for about an hour before use; simply leave the casing covered with clean water in a bowl until you need it. I find that this hydrates the casing and makes it slightly easier to handle.

Open the end of the casing.

Cut the length of casing you need.

Begin to run water through the casing.

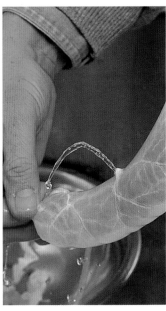

Move the water through the casing.

Look for any leaks in the casing.

Coarse grind using the hand grinder

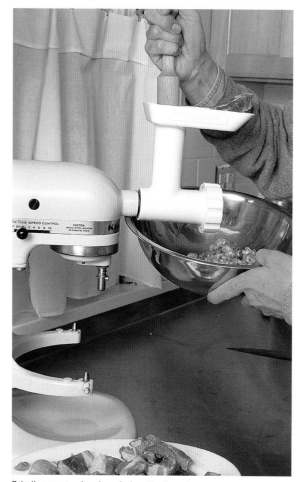

Grinding meat using the grinder attachment

GRINDING, EMULSIFYING, AND HAND CUTTING

Each individual recipe will indicate whether the ingredients need to be ground either coarse or fine, emulsified, or hand-cut. (The Chinese sausage on page 84 calls for the meat and fat to be separately hand diced, and requires no grinding.) If you have followed my advice under Preparing the Meat, and the meat is semifrozen, you should have little difficulty with any of these processes.

Grinding

There are no particular tricks to using a hand grinder or grinder attachment for an electric mixer. Each (see Grinders on page 21) comes with detailed instructions that will explain assembly and how to mount the device.

If the grinder is the sort that clamps onto your counter or worktable, secure it as tightly as you can. Be aware that the jaws of the clamp are often hard enough to damage wood, so I recommend that you place two or three thicknesses of shirt cardboard between the clamp's jaws and your table.

The recipe will tell you whether you need to grind the ingredients coarse or fine and will determine which mincer plate you will use in the grinder. As you become experienced with making sausage, you will develop and understand your own preferences for texture and consistency. I enjoy a chunky consistency in most sausage and will occasionally modify traditional forms to suit myself. Always, please yourself.

You will need to place a receiving bowl beneath the mouth of the grinder. I prefer stainless steel, but ceramic or heavy plastic will do. Be aware that the most important element to consider when choosing utensils is to find those that can be thoroughly cleaned.

Once you've assembled your grinder, either begin turning the handle (clockwise), or start the machine at a slow speed. With your free hand, begin feeding the prepared meat pieces into the hopper on top of your device. Since I've neglected to include any recipes for finger sausage, please be cautious when working any machine, no matter how safe you think it might be.

If you have a stomper, a wooden pestle-like device for pushing meat into the grinding mechanism, use it! Otherwise, be extremely careful when putting meat into the grinder. If the meat or ingredients get stuck when you are using an electric appliance, unplug the machine before beginning your investigation.

Ground meat. **LEFT TO RIGHT**: coarse and fine

Emulsifying

If the recipe requires the filling to be emulsified, you will need to use a food processor, as discussed under Grinders on page 21. Emulsification means that the fat is broken up very finely and distributed evenly throughout the forcemeat. As a point of reference, shaking a bottle of salad dressing to mix the oil with the vinegar emulsifies the solution.

To prepare the meat for emulsification, you will need to cut it into pieces that are small enough to fit in your processor. This means cutting them into pieces smaller than the finger-size pieces suitable for grinding. To emulsify, place the ingredients in the food processor and process the mixture until it resembles a fine-grained paste. As you process, stop occasionally and use a rubber spatula to scrape the sides of the container to ensure that the ingredients process evenly.

Emulsified meat compared to ground meat

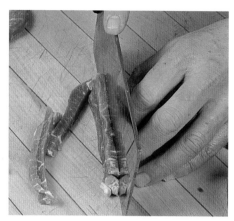

Cut the par-frozen ¼-inch (.6 cm) slabs of meat into ¼-inch strips.

Cut the meat into ¼-inch (.6 cm) dice.

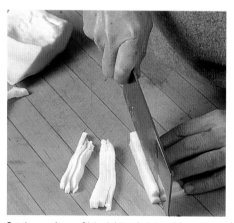

Cut the par-frozen ¼-inch (.6 cm) slabs of fat into ¼-inch strips.

Hand Cutting

The texture of some sausages requires cutting the meat and fat by hand rather than grinding or emulsifying them. When this is the case, the recipe will indicate the size of the dice. If you fancy Italian mortadella, you know that the pieces of fat in the sausage is generally a larger dice. The Chinese sausage on page 84 calls for the meat and fat to be diced fine or small.

When you are hand cutting the meat, it must be semifrozen. When making a small dice you will need to slice the meat into slabs, stack it, cut it into strips, then reorient it, and dice. You will dice the meat and fat separately. Although this process is somewhat tedious compared to grinding, the result is appropriate and wonderful to the style of sausage you are making.

MIXING

Nothing adequately substitutes for using your bare hands for many cooking procedures, and this is one. Aside from providing a guilt-free experience for playing with your food, mixing with your hands provides a second line of defense for finding bone shards and sinew. Make sure you wash your hands well before and after mixing.

As you did for the bulk breakfast sausage on page 14, put all ingredients in a large mixing bowl. Reach across the ingredients, grasp a handful, and push it down through the center of the mass. Turn the bowl a quarter turn and repeat. Continue in this way until all the ingredients are well mixed.

STUFFING

Getting the forcemeat into the casing is the only tricky aspect of sausage making. At first, you may wonder if sausage makers possess a special coordination that you lack. Until you get the feel of it, stuffing sausage is akin to learning how to pat your head and rub your tummy at the same time—it takes the same amount of concentration, and may provide you with the same amount of laughs.

The three phases of stuffing sausage are opening the casing, loading the casing onto the funnel, and packing. With some perseverance, you should have the process perfected after your first batch. Once you have stuffed a sausage, you will know why it is considered a craft.

Opening the Casing

Casings are slippery and need to stay that way if the process is to work. As I mentioned in Preparing the Casings on page 25, I like to keep the casing covered with clean water in a bowl until I need it.

The hardest part of working with casings is finding the opening at the end of the tube. To do this, work in the sink under running water. Let the casing slip through your fingers until you grasp one end. Run water into the end of the casing. You should be able to see and grasp the edge of the tube. This may take several attempts; you can console yourself with the thought that you are developing a useful, though not marketable, skill.

Mix the ingredients by hand.

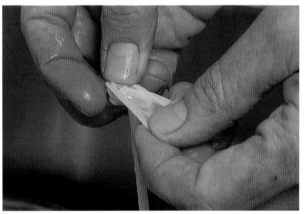
Open the end of the casing.

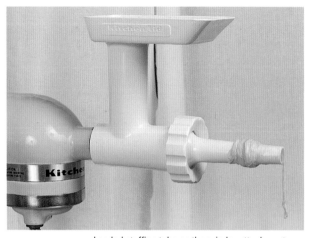

Loaded stuffing tube on the grinder attachment

Loading the Funnel

Now you are ready to *load the funnel*, the term for running the casing onto the outside of the funnel. Your grinder or stuffer should allow you to remove the funnel attachment. Set the funnel on a clean surface with the pointed end facing up. Having opened one end of the casing, gently slide it over the end of the funnel. Hold the trailing portion of the casing in one hand while massaging the casing down over the funnel with the thumb and forefinger of the free hand. This is just like pushing your shirt sleeves up your arm without rolling them (assuming that you were underwater wearing a shirt made out of tissue paper). With practice you will learn how much pressure to use and how tightly to slide the casing on the funnel. To prevent the forcemeat from coming out of the end of the casing as you stuff, tie a simple overhand knot in the casing's end, or use a small piece of kitchen twine to tie off the end.

Loading the stuffing funnel with the casing while the funnel is on a flat surface

Loading the stuffing funnel while working away from a surface

Packing

The last stage of stuffing is packing the forcemeat into the casing. Begin by placing the loaded funnel securely on either the hand grinder, the sausage stuffer, or the grinder attachment for your electric mixer.

If you are using a hand grinder, you may want to consider calling in another pair of hands. Since the hand you use for turning the handle is also the hand you need for placing the forcemeat into the hopper, working alone necessitates that you stop turning the handle while you add more forcemeat. A helper will greatly streamline the process.

A sausage stuffer is designed to hold a substantial volume of forcemeat. Once you load the stuffer's tube, you can concentrate on working the lever with one hand, while guiding the forcemeat into the casing with the other hand.

Tie the end of the casing using an overhand knot or piece of kitchen twine.

Stuffing the sausage with a sausage stuffer

Hold the loaded stuffing tube in your hand to guide the casing off of the tube.

As the forcemeat enters the casing, hold the sausage loosly in your hand while gently pulling the casing back toward the funnel.

Working with the grinder attachment for an electric mixer allows the most ease in packing, since you use one hand for placing the forcemeat into the hopper while the power pushes it into the funnel. You can then easily use the other hand for guiding the forcemeat into the casing.

As the forcemeat is pushed out of whichever device you are using, the pressure will open the casing. As the forcemeat enters the casing, hold the sausage loosely in your hand while gently pulling the casing back toward the funnel; this will give you the control you need to pack the casing firmly or loosely as the recipe recommends (or as you prefer). The casing will burst if the forcemeat is too tightly packed. You will discover how tightly you can pack the casing only by going too far. With practice, you will know exactly how much forcemeat you can pack in.

Stuffing the sausage by hand

Hold the stuffing tube firmly as you push the forcemeat with your thumb.

If you want to make links, it's crucial to *not* overfill the casing at this stage. Keep in mind that in order to twist the sausage every few inches after it is made, you will need to leave some slack in the casing—the only way to do this is to slightly underfill the casing (see Making Links below).

ELIMINATING AIR BUBBLES

It is important to eliminate air bubbles while packing. You will see any large air pockets and bubbles as the forcemeat is being pushed into the casing. You can easily correct this by using your hand to manipulate and rearrange the forcemeat in the casing. In my experience, it is almost impossible to completely eliminate bubbles during the filling stage. The solution is to finish the sausage, then examine it closely. Using a clean needle, prick the bubbles and massage the air out. The small hole made by the needle will not cause the casing to split open when you cook the sausage.

Remove any air pockets by piercing them with a clean needle.

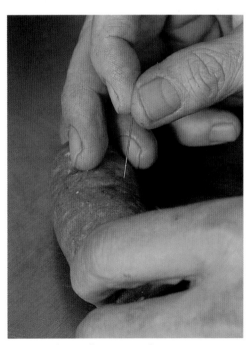

Using a sewing needle to remove air pockets from a chorizo sausage

Lay the sausage on a flat surface and twist into links.

Making Links

Some butchers use elaborate methods (many passed down through the generations) for tying off links. I found that a few twists between links will effectively hold them together while giving you enough casing to cut when you want to separate the links. To make links, first lay the stuffed sausage on a work surface. Starting at one end of the sausage, begin to measure, then twist the sausage to make the size links you want. Do not attempt to twist the links as the sausage is coming off the funnel. By placing the sausage flat on a surface before twisting, the links will not unroll. If you are going to poach the sausages immediately after they are made, you may want to tie short lengths of kitchen twine between each link. This provides a little extra security to prevent the links from unrolling as you place them in the pot for poaching.

Do not make the links this way—they will come untwisted. It's always better to work on a flat surface.

Use short lengths of kitchen twine to tie off the twists between links.

SANITATION

You cannot overstress the importance of proper sanitation when making sausage. Most cooking involves risks of contamination, and meats in particular provide potential for food poisoning and a vector for serious (and very highly publicized though actually quite rare) diseases such as Escherichia coli (*e. coli*), trichinosis, and botulism. My response to the risks is to be scrupulous with the following rules:

- Thoroughly wash all utensils and work surfaces that come in contact with meats with hot, soapy water. Try to avoid cross contamination by always rinsing your cloth or sponge in the hot soapy water *after* cleaning a surface or utensil, *before* you wipe another surface or utensil with the same cloth or sponge.

- If equipment can be disassembled, always take it apart and separately clean those piece that have come in contact with the food. It's always best to rinse or immerse implements in boiling water after they have been thoroughly cleaned.

- Never reuse work surfaces without washing after each process.

- A cursory wiping is not sufficient to clean and sanitize the surface. Again, use hot soapy water and a well-rinsed cloth or sponge.

- Never store meats in the vessels in which they have been prepared. Small particles of unseasoned meat left in vessels after preparation could be a breeding ground for bacteria when left at room temperature. When you reintroduce your prepared mixture, these small particles could contaminate the entire batch.

- Keep all ingredients as cold as possible. If you need to do further preparation or need to leave the kitchen for any length of time, place the ingredients or the meat mixture into the refrigerator.

- Always cook sausage thoroughly. This, in itself, is a skill often learned by trial and error involving one too many overly done sausages. While you don't want to undercook the sausages, you don't want to overcook them either (see below).

Cleaning supplies

Sterilizing utensils with boiling water

Sausages ready to dry in the refrigerator. Note the bowl under the rack to catch the liquid. You may also use a colander placed over a pan.

Some recipes call for sautéed crumbled sausage. (See recipe on page 97.)

STORAGE AND COOKING

Link sausages benefit from a bit of drying which allows them to brown nicely during frying or grilling. Once you've made your fresh sausage, arrange the links so they do not touch each other. Some recipes call for you to cover them, others do not. You may want to place them on a rack in a shallow pan to allow the pan to catch any drippings from the sausage. Store them overnight in the refrigerator.

Having dried them, you can then cook them in any one of several ways (see below), or wrap them in butcher paper or wax paper and refrigerate the sausages for up to three days. To freeze, dry the sausage overnight as above, then place the sausage in a freezer bag (removing as much air as you can before sealing) and freeze for up to three months. To thaw, place them in the refrigerator for a day.

The method you choose for cooking depends on your own pleasure. I love the texture of fried or grilled sausage—they are beautifully brown, crack out loud when you bite into them, and the juices burst in your mouth. Unless I plan to serve sausages cold (there is no better reason to make a sandwich than cold sausage), I always try to serve them immediately off the grill or stove; the longer they sit, the more the juices will soften the crisp skins. For some meals I prefer poached sausage for the moist result and the way the texture complements other ingredients and sauces. When sausage is to be added to a soup, such as the earthy Caldo Verde on page 96, I prefer the poaching method.

When you are ready to cook your sausages, try the following approaches. The directions assume you are cooking sausages stuffed into hog casings that are approximately 1 to 1½ inches (2.5 to 4 cm) wide. You will need to adjust your cooking time for any sausages that are less than 1 inch (2.5 cm) or more than 2 inches (5 cm) in diameter. Enjoy each of the methods, remembering that variety is not the hobgoblin of great cooking.

Baking

I generally prefer other methods of cooking sausage; however, baking is a great solution for cooking for a large gathering. Furthermore, baking sausage for a long time over very low heat is an alternate method of making a sausage that approximates the texture and flavors of dried sausages such as salami.

Should you wish to bake sausage for a meal, preheat your oven to 300°F (150°C). Arrange the sausages on a rack over a pan to catch the drippings. Using a fork or needle, prick each link several times. Bake for 45 minutes; the juices should be quite clear when done.

Crumbled Sausage

Many dishes call for crumbled sausage, which is fried first and then added to the remaining ingredients—or even assembled at the table, such as make-your-own tacos. To prepare sausage this way, remove the casing from the sausage before cooking. I find it easiest to cook the sausage using a wooden spoon that breaks up the meat into small pieces as they fry. During cooking, the fat melts out from the meat and forms the ideal cooking medium for these morsels. Some dishes ask you to remove and reserve the meat, allowing you to use some of the sausage fat for cooking (and seasoning) other ingredients.

Frying

Place the sausage links in a pan that is large enough to hold them in a single layer without them touching each other. Use a fork or needle to prick each sausage four or five times. Just barely cover the links with cold water and bring to a boil. Lower the heat immediately and simmer for 10 minutes. If foam forms, skim it. If the sausage floats, turn them halfway through the simmering. After the 10 minutes are up, pour off the remaining water. Again, prick each sausage two or

easy cleaning

A lick-and-a-promise cleaning is no longer suitable for today's discriminating cooks who are fearful of e. coli and salmonella contamination. While proper use of hot soapy water is sufficient for cleaning home food preparation areas, you can provide an extra measure of cleanliness by making your own inexpensive spray from bleach and water. Simply mix one teaspoon of bleach with 32 ounces (.95 L) of water. Once you've cleaned with hot soapy water, spray the bleach solution on desired surfaces and let stand for a few minutes. Then rinse the surface and air dry, or use paper towels to pat the surface dry. You will smell the bleach when it is wet; however, since so little bleach is used, it will dissipate over time and will not affect future food preparation.

Spray bottle with bleach solution

Split and grilled merguez sausage (recipe on page 86)

To poach, place the sausage in enough water to cover by at least 1 inch (2.5 cm).

three times to release some of the fat. Be careful at this point because the fat is under some pressure and may shoot out. If you do not get enough sausage fat from piercing the sausages to coat the pan with a thin film of fat, add a little olive or vegetable oil to prevent the sausage from sticking. Raise the heat to medium and brown the sausages on all sides—this should take approximately three minutes.

Grilling

There are no tricks to grilling sausage except satisfying each guest's particular preference for level of burn. I like to poach mine lightly so they hold together during the initial cooking stage, and to ensure that the links are cooked through before they are blackened on the outside. The casing tends to stick to the grill and tear. If this bothers you, I recommend one of those hinged grilling frames used for delicate foods. When one side is properly crisp, you invert the whole device to grill the other side. Alternatively, you can brush the links with a bit of vegetable oil to keep them from sticking.

Poaching

Using a fork or needle, prick each sausage link a few times. If you have a steamer or pasta insert, place it in a pot large enough to hold all of the sausage you wish to poach. Add enough cold water to cover the sausage by at least 1 inch (2.5 cm).

Over high heat, bring the liquid just to the point where the first bubbles appear—you never want to let the liquid come to a boil, since this will toughen the sausage. Immediately reduce the heat to the lowest setting, add the sausage, cover the pot, and let simmer for 20 minutes. If the sausage begins to float, place a plate on it while it simmers to keep the sausage in the water. After 20 minutes you can serve or chill.

NOTE: Over the years I have developed some cooking habits that form my personal kitchen style. For example, if ever a recipe requires boiling or poaching (in any liquid, including wine, stock, water, or beer), I always throw in some aromatic vegetables, such as carrots, onions, garlic, celery, a piece of ginger, a slice of lemon peel, a bay leaf—or all of the above. This not only gently flavors the sausage, but makes an easy and delicious stock. Because of the fat content of the sausage, remember to thoroughly degrease this stock before use.

Smoking

There are a wide variety of smokers on the market, and you may already own one. We referred earlier to hot smoking (see page 76) as a method of extending the shelf life of sausage. Here, we are looking at the smoker as a method of cooking. Each type of smoker will have its own slight variations in the smoking process, but one main issue remains the same. That is, you need a temperature hot enough to cook the sausage thoroughly and low enough to keep them from charring before they are smoked.

SMOKING GUIDELINES

The links should be dry. Build and light the charcoal fire, and let it burn down to a smooth gray ash. It should reach a temperature of about 275°F (135°C). Place soaked wood chips on the prepared charcoal. Install the filled water bowl and, above that, the grids with the sausage. Close the smoker, and monitor the temperature to control the speed of cooking. With a chef's thermometer (one that will register the temperature instantly) check for an internal temperature of 170°F (78°C). This should take approximately three to five hours. Always refer to your smoker's manual and the recipes.

While poaching, never let water boil, but simmer for specified time.

You may need to weight down the poaching sausages with a plate to keep them submerged in the water as they cook.

recipes for great sausages

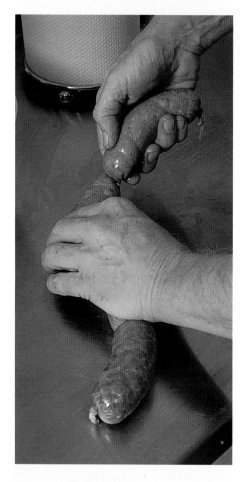

an international experience

MANY OF US REFER TO SAUSAGES BY THE COUNTRY FROM WHICH THEY CAME. I was raised by a pair of otherwise sophisticated cooks who talked broadly of Polish, Italian, Portuguese, or German sausage, rather than of the astounding variety within these cuisines. I have finally discovered what some of you may already know, that kielbasa is not actually a type of sausage, as in Polish kielbasa, but merely a Polish word for all sausage.

The more I learn of international cuisine the greater the richness and variety becomes apparent to me. I mentioned earlier the 600 sausage varieties described in *The Great Book of Sausages*. Within this survey is listed 118 varieties of French, 108 German, 65 English, and 40 Italian sausages.

I have organized the following sausage recipes by country. I have chosen many of my favorite sausages and have also introduced myself to varieties that I had never tried, such as Chinese and Swedish potato sausage. All have been winners.

For the purposes of this book I have limited my recipes to those that can be made with commonly available ingredients. I have always found it frustrating to be told of a transcendent dish only to discover that the ingredient that elevates the food heavenward is unavailable in my hemisphere.

Keep in mind that the goal of this (and I believe any) cookbook is to provide you with two things that should lead you to a third. First, I have tried to give you a decent background in the concept and general theory. Second, I want to provide you with experience in making your own sausage through these recipes. Finally, having obtained the theory and practice of home sausage making, I hope you will branch out and develop your own variations. You'll soon find what textures please you most, how intensely you like your sausage spiced and flavored, and how much fat you need to reach the balance you prefer.

Allow your imagination to be limited only by the seasons and the availability of great ingredients. Take advantage of your own garden, your cousin who hunts, the farmer's market in your town. Shop for the most beautiful produce in its season.

Try something you've never tasted. If you never had quite enough garlic in your sausage, push the limits. Try ostrich meat or add raisins and dried mango to a curried lamb mixture. I'm not a great fan of tofu, however, it offers fun possibilities for meatless sausage with olive oil as the fat. I say, cry havoc and let loose the hot dogs of boar (or soy).

the sausages

ITALY
salsiccie
luganega
cotechino
mortadella

FRANCE
saucisson a l'ail
boudin blanc
boudin blanc aux pommes
cervelas aux pistache

GREAT BRITAIN
bangers
oyster sausage

IBERIA AND MEXICO
linguiça
butifarra
chorizo

SCANDINAVIA
julkorv
ingefarapolse
medvurst
kaalikaaryleet
riismakkara

GERMANY
bockwurst
bratwurst
liverwurst
vienna sausage

ASIA, THE MIDDLE EAST, AND GREECE
lop cheong
si klok
merguez
keftedakia

UNITED STATES
hot dogs
cajun boudin
southern country sausage

italy

EVERY CUISINE OFFERS AT LEAST A FEW SUPREME ACCOMPLISHMENTS.
Italy has, of course, retired the trophy. I require the fruit of all cuisines for my happiness to be complete; however, if I *had to choose* one and only one culinary source, I would not hesitate to choose Italy.

Italy is the one country that, I believe, best understands the principles of feeding—whether it involves feeding themselves, feeding their guests, or feeding their identities. It is characteristic of Italian life that each village and city believes that it, and it alone, truly understands rice, or fish, or fungi… or sausage (even though there are perhaps fewer named types of sausage in Italy than in France or Germany).

If ever a war was fought over sausage, it would be in this country. Often the only difference between the garlic sausage in one village and that of the next is the lineage of the pig. Those of us who are not of Italy born can only travel through the country and reap the bounty of the argument.

I once spent a Bohemian summer in Hamburg (this is not an oxymoron…I simply mean I was poor and artistic) working in a kitchen as a *plongeur* (French for pearl diver…you know, a dishwasher). I was part of a wonderfully motley society of others, auslandern, who spoke no common language except a very rudimentary German. In order to communicate we created a patois such that any given sentence included German, French, Italian, English, and Spanish words strung together in a vaguely Teutonic syntax.

The two most vocal of our group were Giuseppe and Luighi, both Roman. They gave me the reverence I have held ever since for the food of Italy. They actually wept in misery over the food we were given twice daily as part of our pay. It would not have been considered bad by most of America in the 1950s mind you, being a little bland and a little too efficient. Once a week we were served a large mound of boiled rice with boiled chicken necks in white sauce. It was definitely fuel, not food—enough to keep us going until we were freed at midnight.

Throughout the summer, Giuseppe would lecture us on the Italian attitude toward food, while Luighi would supply the sound effects—moaning, slurping, and various other noises connoting ecstasy and disdain. We learned that as important as punctuality was to the German, so was food to the Italian. They claimed that, in Italy, the poorest people ate well.

From these impromptu and entertaining (thanks to Luighi) talks, I gleaned two bits of information that continue to guide me when I cook Italian (or otherwise). First, it is important that each ingredient be of high quality. And second, that the integrity of those ingredients is a hallmark; flavors must never be buried underneath other flavors but each allowed to sing its own essential note.

Grilled Italian
salsiccie (recipe next
page), served with
peppers in olive oil
(recipe page 123)

SALSICCIE

Salsiccie is a basic Italian sausage, and is closest to what we in the U.S. think of as Italian sausage. Stewed with green peppers in a red sauce, this defines the "Little Italy" in many American cities.

This recipe is very satisfying to me, and I've produced it in a larger than normal quantity. I believe that it is one of the great basic sausages, and you *need* to always keep some in your freezer. Various regional differences can be approximated by substituting coriander or anise for the fennel seed, adding thyme, vermouth, or cayenne.

INGREDIENTS

5 pounds (2.27 kg) pork butt, boned and trimmed of sinew

OR,

4 pounds (1.8 kg) lean pork loin and 1 pound (448 g) unsalted pork fat

2½ teaspoons sea salt

1 tablespoon (heaping) of black pepper, or a generous grinding

1 tablespoon whole fennel seed

Crushed red pepper to taste (use for hot sausage, omit for sweet sausage)

5 feet (1.8 m) of prepared hog casing

METHOD

Par freeze the meat and fat. You will need to work quickly to keep the ingredients chilled. Have the grinder and stuffing attachments sterile and assembled. Load the casing onto the stuffing horn and set aside. Have all ingredients ready and arrayed adjacent to your work surface.

Slice the meat and fat into 1-inch (2.5 cm) slabs. Stack the slabs, then cut again into finger-size pieces. Grind the meat and fat together using the coarse disk for your grinder or grinder attachment.

In a large mixing bowl that has been thoroughly cleaned in soapy water and scalded with boiling water, mix the meat and fat with all remaining ingredients. Using your hands to mix, reach across the ingredients, grasp a handful, and push it down through the center of the mass. Turn bowl a quarter turn and repeat. Continue until well mixed.

Stuff the completed forcemeat firmly into the casings. You may leave the sausage in coils or twist the finished sausage into 3- to 6-inch (7.5 to 15 cm) links. If you will be making links, remember to leave some slack in the casing by understuffing slightly to prevent the casing from bursting when you twist the sausage.

If you will be cooking the sausage within three days, arrange on sheet pans and refrigerate, uncovered, overnight to dry the skins. Then cook, or wrap and store the sausages in the refrigerator until ready to cook. Freeze the remainder of the sausage in meal-sized portions by first wrapping the portions in butcher or wax paper, then placing the wrapped portion in freezer bags from which you remove as much air as possible.

This sausage keeps in the freezer for three months. They will be perfectly safe if you leave them in the freezer longer, but their flavor may begin to fade. When you wish to defrost sausage, place the package in the refrigerator overnight before unwrapping.

YIELD: Approximatley 5 pounds (2.27 kg) of sausage

LUGANEGA

This delicious northern Italian sausage is made without the ubiquitous fennel seed. The parmesan cheese and white wine give this sausage a subtle bite with mellow overtones. If you've only eaten Italian sausage with fennel seed, make this sausage!

INGREDIENTS

2½ pounds (1.12 kg) pork butt, boned and trimmed of sinew

OR,

2 pounds (896 g) lean pork loin and ½ pound (224 g) unsalted pork fat

½ cup (60 g) grated Parmesan cheese

½ teaspoon sea salt

½ tablespoon of white pepper

¼ cup (60 mL) dry white wine

1 tablespoon minced fresh oregano (if using dry oregano, use 1½ teaspoons)

2 cloves fresh garlic, finely minced

4 feet (1.2 m) of prepared hog casing

METHOD

Par freeze the meat and fat. You will need to work quickly to keep the ingredients chilled. Have the grinder and stuffing attachments sterile and assembled. Load the casing onto the stuffing horn and set aside. Have all ingredients ready and arrayed adjacent to your work surface.

Slice the meat and fat into 1-inch (2.5 cm) slabs. Stack the slabs, then cut again into finger-size pieces. Grind the meat and fat together using the coarse disk for your grinder or grinder attachment.

In a large mixing bowl that has been thoroughly cleaned in soapy water and scalded with boiling water, mix the meat and fat with all remaining ingredients. Using your hands, reach across the ingredients, grasp a handful, and push it down through the center of the mass. Turn bowl a quarter turn and repeat. Continue until well mixed.

Stuff the completed forcemeat firmly into the casings. You may leave the sausage in coils or twist the finished sausage into 3- to 6-inch (7.5 to 15 cm) links. If you will be making links, remember to leave some slack in the casing by understuffing slightly to prevent the casing from bursting when you twist the sausage.

If you will be cooking the sausage within three days, arrange on sheet pans and refrigerate, uncovered, overnight to dry the skins. Then cook, or wrap and store the sausages in the refrigerator until ready to cook. Freeze the remainder of the sausage in meal-sized portions by first wrapping the portions in butcher or wax paper, then placing the wrapped portion in freezer bags from which you remove as much air as possible.

This sausage keeps in the freezer for three months. They will be perfectly safe if you leave them in the freezer longer, but their flavor may begin to fade. When you wish to defrost sausage, place the package in the refrigerator overnight before unwrapping.

YIELD: Approximately 3 pounds (1.35 kg) of sausage

COTECHINO

Cotechino has always been a rare treat for me (like sweetbreads, I will always order it when I find it on a menu). The combination of nutmeg, cinnamon, and cloves gives it a distinct spicy flavor. Served with a light lemon sauce and stewed lentils, it is simply wonderful. This is an important New Year's dish in Rome, where the lentils symbolize coins to portend a prosperous year, and the large, fresh, garlic sausage is often stuffed and tied in a boned pig's foot (in which case, it is called Zampone). Barring that, cotechino are typically large sausages stuffed into bungs. This recipe calls for the more easily available hog casings.

INGREDIENTS

- 5 pounds (2.27 kg) of fresh ham, boned and trimmed of sinew
- 1 pound (448 g) of the skin and fat from the ham
- ¼ cup (30 g) of grated Parmesan cheese
- 3 teaspoons sea salt
- 4 teaspoons ground pepper
- ¼ cup (60 mL) dry white wine
- 1 teaspoon cayenne
- 2 teaspoons ground nutmeg
- 2 teaspoons ground cinnamon
- 1 teaspoon ground cloves
- 5 cloves fresh garlic, finely minced
- 5 feet (1.5 m) of prepared hog casing

METHOD

Par freeze the meat and fat. You will need to work quickly to keep the ingredients chilled. Have the grinder and stuffing attachments sterile and assembled. Load the casing onto the stuffing horn and set aside. Have all ingredients ready and arrayed adjacent to your work surface.

Slice the meat and fat into 1-inch (2.5 cm) slabs. Stack the slabs, then cut again into finger-size pieces. Grind the meat and fat together using the coarse disk for your grinder or grinder attachment.

Mix the meat and fat with all remaining ingredients. Grind this mixture a second time, using the fine disk for your grinder or grinder attachment.

Stuff the completed forcemeat firmly into the casings. You may leave the sausage in coils or twist the finished sausage into 3- to 6-inch (7.5 to 15 cm) links. If you will be making links, remember to leave some slack in the casing by understuffing slightly to prevent the casing from bursting when you twist the sausage.

If you will be cooking the sausage within three days, arrange on sheet pans and refrigerate, uncovered, overnight to dry the skins. Then cook, or wrap and store the sausages in the refrigerator until ready to cook. Freeze the remainder of the sausage in meal-sized portions by first wrapping the portions in butcher or wax paper, then placing the wrapped portion in freezer bags from which you remove as much air as possible.

TIP: You may also store these sausages by making a kind of confit, which is meat preserved in solidified fat. To do this, poach the links for 45 minutes, then cool them thoroughly. Place them in a canning jar, and cover them with hot melted fat. You can keep them in the refrigerator for up to two weeks. To serve, reheat the sausages, draining off the fat.

YIELD: Approximatley 6 pounds (2.72 kg) of sausage

cotechino's cousin

Zampone is cotechino stuffed into a boned pig's foot—the word zampa being Italian for pig's foot. Legend has it that this delicacy came about in the 16th century when Modena, its city of origin, was besieged, and the residents could only find pigs' hooves to use as casings for their sausage.

MORTADELLA

In my search for great food with which to feed my friends and family, there are several cooks on whom I know that I can rely. One of these is Marcella Hazan. Although she seems to doubt very much that I will ever be able to find edible ingredients outside of Italy, I have been unfailingly successful with her recipes. One such recipe has become an autumn favorite of mine, Capellacci del Nuovo Mundo, or, pasta stuffed with sweet potatoes. This surprising dish calls for mortadella, the aristocrat of bolognas, which is a large, smooth, pink, pre-cooked sausage unctuous with little islands of snowy fat and studded with peppercorns.

For this mortadella to be authentic, you will need a food processor to emulsify most of the fat and to create a forcemeat that is very fine grained. Also, to be strictly correct, you will need hog bungs or muslin bags (see page 80) to make the sausage as wide as you can, at least 3 inches (7.5 cm). However, you can make it in hog casings. Finally, to achieve the pinkness that we associate with all bolognas, they should be smoked. As an alternative, you can bake them as described below. Enjoy!

INGREDIENTS

- 3 pounds (1.36 kg) of lean pork
- ¾ pound (336 g) of pork fat
- 3 garlic cloves
- 1 teaspoon ground mace
- ¼ teaspoon ground cloves
- ¼ cup (60 mL) dry white wine (such as vermouth)
- 2 tablespoons sea salt
- 1 teaspoon liquid smoke (omit if you will be smoking these)
- 1 teaspoon coriander seeds
- ½ cup (56 g) unsalted, shelled pistachios
- 1½ teaspoons whole peppercorns (or more, I like to mix black and green peppercorns in a ratio of 2 to 1)
- 5 feet (1.5 m) of prepared hog casings, or hog bungs or muslin bags

METHOD

Set aside one-third of the fat and cut it into ¼-inch (.6 cm) cubes. Prepare the remainder of the fat and the meat by cutting them into pieces that are small enough to fit in your food processor. Working in manageable batches, put the remainder of the fat and the meat into your food processor that is fitted with a steel blade, and process until completely smooth. When finished, the mixture should be a fine-grained paste.

Add the garlic, mace, cloves, wine, salt, and liquid smoke (if not smoking the sausage in a smoker) to the emulsified meat and fat mixture, and reprocess in the food processor until all the ingredients are well blended. Place the forcemeat in a mixing bowl, and carefully add all remaining ingredients and the fat that has been cut into ¼-inch (.6 cm) cubes. Mix gently but thoroughly.

Stuff the completed forcemeat firmly into the casings. You may leave the sausage in coils or twist into 3- to 6-inch (7.5 to 15 cm) links. Remember, if you are preparing the sausage for links, leave enough slack in the casing by slightly understuffing to prevent the casing from bursting as you twist.

If you are leaving the sausage in a coil, and before you make links, search for air pockets, prick them with a clean needle, and massage the air out. If you are using a muslin bag, follow the stuffing instructions for Liverwurst on page 80.

If you are using a smoker, cook the mortadella at 275°F (135°C) until it reaches an internal temperature of 170°F (77°C). If you are not using a smoker, place the sausage on a baking sheet and cook the sausage by baking at 200°F (95°C) for 5 hours. Once the mortadella is either smoked or baked, wrap and refrigerate it, where it will keep for two weeks.

YIELD: Approximately 4 pounds (1.8 kg) of sausage

making poultry sausage

Over the past several years, poultry sausage has become very popular in the U.S. Wide varieties are offered in gourmet shops and markets. These products can be excellent, and are typically much lower in fat than those produced from their hoofed brethren. However, when thinking of making poultry sausage, keep in mind this rule of thumb: Low fat can mean dry sausage.

While you can add some pork fat to moisten poultry sausage, it is better (and more common) to use poultry fat and the skin, which you grind into your mixture, as the fat source. Furthermore, dark meat is much more flavorful than white meat. I prefer a mixture of chicken and turkey thighs, which I bone in advance and freeze for future use in 1-pound (.45 kg) portions. Until you have boned poultry a few times, you may find this a little tedious. If you are starting out, you may want to work with a small quantity at first, then build up a reserve over time.

A particularly tasty sausage can be made from free-range chickens, turkeys, ducks, geese, or game birds. Free-range birds exercise all of their muscles, which bathes the flesh in blood and enriches its flavor. Since free-range birds are leaner, you won't get as much fat from the thighs as you would from commercially raised birds, so feel free to include the breast meat if you like. As a side note: Duck and goose fat is extraordinarily unctuous and will produce very moist sausage. Also, as a cooking medium, I prefer it to butter since it burns at a much higher temperature—so even if you don't use it in sausage, save it (or send it to me!).

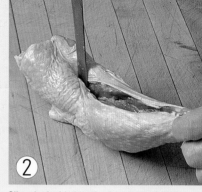

1 Remove the bottom of the bone.

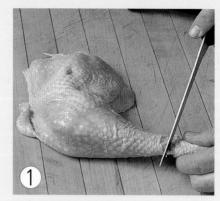

2 Slice the inside length of the leg and thigh.

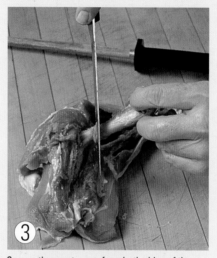

3 Scrape the meat away from both sides of the bones, then remove the bones.

4 Cut the meat away from the tendons.

5 Remove the tendons.

6 Remove the sheet tendons.

PURE POULTRY SAUSAGE
WITH YUCATAN SEASONING

The Yucatan Peninsula is one of my favorite spots on earth. The sun, ancient stone ruins, the ocean—all conspire to put me in a hammock. Sooner or later, I find myself nibbling on appetizers called botanas (spicy pickled onions, carrots, and garlic cloves) waiting for something with cilantro, chilies, and lime juice. Sounds good? Then try these.

INGREDIENTS

- 2 pounds (896 g) boned chicken or turkey thighs with skin
- 1 cup (180 g) onion, minced
- 2 tablespoons vegetable oil
- 2 cloves fresh garlic, minced
- ½ bunch fresh cilantro, leaves only, roughly chopped
- 1 serrano pepper, minced and seeded
- 1 teaspoon salt
- ½ teaspoon allspice, ground
- ½ teaspoon cumin, ground
- ¼ teaspoon cinnamon, ground
- 1 tablespoons sundried tomatoes, soaked in water and minced
-   Juice of 1 lime
- 4 feet (1.2 m) of prepared hog casing

METHOD

If not already done, bone the chicken or turkey thighs (see page 48). Par freeze the meat with skin. Have the grinder and stuffing attachments sterile and assembled. Load the casing onto the stuffing horn and set aside. Have all ingredients ready and arrayed adjacent to your work surface.

Slice the meat with skin into 1-inch (2.5 cm) slabs. Stack the slabs, then cut again into finger-size pieces. Grind the meat and skin using the coarse disk for your grinder or grinder attachment.

In a large mixing bowl that has been thoroughly cleaned in soapy water and scalded with boiling water, use your hands to mix the ground meat with all remaining ingredients.

Stuff the completed forcemeat firmly into the casings. Twist the sausage into 4- to 6-inch (10 to 15 cm) links. Since you will be making links, remember to leave some slack in the casing by understuffing slightly to prevent the casing from bursting when you twist the sausage. Remove any air pockets by piercing with a clean needle.

Poach the sausage for 30 minutes (see the directions for poaching on page 38). Prepare and eat immediately, or cool, wrap, and store in the refrigerator for five days, or in the freezer for three months.

YIELD: Approximately 2½ pounds (1.12 kg) of sausage

THE NOTION OF FRENCH FOOD IS TOO OFTEN TAKEN EXCLUSIVELY TO INDICATE HIGH SOPHISTICATION. Yet haute cuisine does not even come close to telling the story of this rich tradition. Peasant food, cooked and eaten by those who grow it—*that* forms the spine of the great foods of France. These include intense, rich stews, pot-au-feu or cassoulet (white beans cooked with garlic sausage and preserved duck), and choucroute garnie, the autumn glory of Alsace with braised sweet sauerkraut served with a variety of meats and sausage.

Sausage is peasant food, the richly flavored and ingenious use of "the rest of the beast" left after the farmer has sold the expensive cuts—the tenderloins and rib roasts of beef and pork, and the loin lamb and veal chops. France is known for having more different cheeses than the days of the year, and they could be equally renowned for their variety of sausage.

There are basic types of French sausage: Andouille, andouilletes, boudins noir and blanc, gallantines, crepinettes, saucisson, saucisette, and on and on. Of each type, there are many regional variations. I won't go into all of them, but I will share some history and sausiculture (to coin a word).

One of the signature French sausages, andouillette, consists primarily of one section of pigs' intestines stuffed into another. In a treatise on the French language (written by Henry VIII's Chaplain) the 16th century French word for the section to be stuffed is *endoile*. It comes as a shock for many Americans to learn that the word's early English equivalent was *chyterling*. If you know about cuisine in the southern United States, this should start to sound familiar. To further trace this sausage's lineage, Louisiana's wonderful, spicy Cajun sausage that is a requirement for red beans and rice and many gumbos is called *andouille*.

Back in France it seems that finding the andouille's lineage is not as straightforward. The authors of the survey volume, *The Great Book of Sausages*, found themselves as judges at the annual festival of the society of andouille lovers, known as *La Confrérie des Chevaliers du Goûte-Andouille*. (In France, there are at least two other national associations of friends, or actually knights, of the andouille.) During this festival the Coxes were asked to judge among 80 examples of these delicacies. They report that they were defeated by the task, having made it through only 44 samples of every imaginable permutation of basic ingredients. Just contemplating so many different varieties of one sausage, you must admit, is an indication that France takes its sausage seriously.

One more factoid before we can make some French sausage. The enormous volume, *Larousse Gastronimique, Encyclopedia of Food, Wines and Cookery* by Prosper Montagné has several pages referring to boudins (which also have a Cajun variation). Montagné tells us that boudin noir (a blood sausage) comes to us as a dish very little altered from that produced by the Assyrian pork butchers of Tyre. Among several recipes, one is reproduced in verse as it was written by the French cook/poet Achille Ozanne. This recipe is, unfortunately, neither useful instruction nor good poetry. Merely, that it was written and is preserved speaks volumes. And so, on to the good stuff…

French cassoulet
provides a hearty,
tasty one-dish
meal. (recipe on
page 111)

SAUCISSON A L'AIL
GARLIC SAUSAGE

I consider this a quintessentially Gallic sausage. My approach calls for twice the amount of garlic that you might find in other cookbooks, but still less than you might find in a French charcuterie.

During the 1970s and `80s, I lived in Washington, D.C., where the French community was large enough to support a terrific shop called "The French Market." They made the most redolently garlic sausages I had ever tasted. While my culinary courage has occasionally taken me places I will not return, in this case I became a convert. These sausages stood up to the stewing process and partnered with the white beans and preserved duck in the most warming cassoulet I had eaten. Magnificent!

INGREDIENTS

5½ pounds (2.48 kg) of pork butt, boned and trimmed of sinew

OR,

4 pounds (1.8 kg) lean pork loin and 1½ pounds (672 g) unsalted pork fat

1 tablespoon sea salt

1 teaspoon white pepper

1 teaspoon thyme

1 cup (240 mL) cognac

1 bay leaf, minced

5 cloves fresh garlic, finely minced

7 feet (2.3 m) of prepared hog casing

METHOD

Par freeze the meat and fat. You will need to work quickly to keep the ingredients chilled. Have the grinder and stuffing attachments sterile and assembled. Load the casing onto the stuffing horn and set aside. Have all ingredients ready and arrayed adjacent to your work surface.

Slice the meat and fat into 1-inch (2.5 cm) slabs. Stack the slabs, then cut again into finger-size pieces. Grind the meat and fat together using the coarse disk for your grinder or grinder attachment.

In a large mixing bowl that has been thoroughly cleaned in soapy water and scalded with boiling water, mix the meat and fat with all remaining ingredients. Using your hands, reach across the ingredients, grasp a handful, and push it down through the center of the mass. Turn bowl a quarter turn and repeat. Continue until well mixed.

Stuff the completed forcemeat firmly into the casings. You may leave the sausage in coils or twist the finished sausage into 3- to 6-inch (7.5–15 cm) links. If you will be making links, remember to leave some slack in the casing by understuffing slightly to prevent the casing from bursting when you twist the sausage.

If you will be cooking the sausage within three days, arrange on sheet pans and refrigerate, uncovered, overnight to dry the skins. Then cook, or wrap and store the sausages in the refrigerator until ready to cook. Freeze the remainder of the sausage in meal-sized portions by first wrapping the portions in butcher or wax paper, then placing the wrapped portion in freezer bags from which you remove as much air as possible.

This sausage keeps in the freezer for three months. They will be perfectly safe if you leave them in the freezer longer, but their flavor may begin to fade. When you wish to defrost sausage, place the package in the refrigerator overnight before unwrapping.

YIELD: Approximately 5½ pounds (2.48 kg) of sausage

BOUDIN BLANC

Boudin blanc is perhaps the most common sausage in France. Many of them, like this recipe, mix poultry with pork. Where rabbits are plentiful, they are used as well. It is a Christmas and New Year's tradition to serve a version of these very delicate sausages flecked with truffles. If you are feeling flush, buy a small jar or can of black truffles, mince them finely and add them, with their juice, to the sausage mixture.

INGREDIENTS

- ½ pound (224 g) lean pork
- ½ pound (224 g) skinless and boneless chicken breast
- ½ pound (224 g) unsalted pork fat
- 1 small onion, roughly chopped
- 1 tablespoon butter
- 1 cup (240 mL) heavy cream
- ½ cup (115 g) tightly packed, good, white French bread torn into small pieces
- ½ teaspoon of an equal mixture of ground cloves, coriander, and nutmeg
- 1½ teaspoons sea salt
- ¼ teaspoon white pepper
- 1 large whole egg
- 1 egg white
- 3 feet (.9 m) of prepared hog casing

METHOD

Par freeze the meats and fat. Have the grinder and stuffing attachments sterile and assembled. Load the casing onto the stuffing horn and set aside. Have all ingredients ready and arrayed adjacent to your work surface.

Cook the onion in butter until translucent (do not brown), and set aside to cool. Scald (but do not boil) the cream. Pour the cream over the bread that is in a small bowl, and stir in spices, salt, and pepper.

Slice the meats and fat into 1-inch (2.5 cm) slabs. Stack the slabs, then cut again into finger-size pieces. Grind the meats and fat together using the coarse disk for your grinder or grinder attachment.

In a large mixing bowl that has been thoroughly cleaned in soapy water and scalded with boiling water, mix the meat and fat with all remaining ingredients, including the onion and the cream-soaked bread. Using you hands, reach across the ingredients, grasp a handful, and push it down through the center of the mass. Turn bowl a quarter turn and repeat. Continue until well mixed.

Stuff the completed forcemeat firmly into the casings. Twist the finished sausage into 3- to 6-inch (7.5 to 15 cm) links. Since you will be making links, remember to leave some slack in the casing by understuffing slightly to prevent the casing from bursting when you twist the sausage. Remove any air bubbles by pricking them with a clean needle.

NOTE: Since this sausage is so delicate, it is best cooked and eaten soon after making it. I suggest that you simply grill it, then serve them with mashed potatoes and a green salad.

YIELD: Approximately 2 pounds (896 g) of sausage

BOUDIN BLANC AUX POMMES
APPLE SAUSAGE

These are among my favorites. If you like to offer tastings with varieties of sausage (as do I), this is one you must include. It is a Norman specialty made with apples, butter, and Calvados, an apple brandy. It is made with half pork and half chicken, and can be made with all chicken if you like. Poach these sausages after stuffing, then heat them through to serve. Another method of serving is to skin them carefully after poaching, roll them in bread crumbs, then fry them in butter until browned.

INGREDIENTS

½ pound (224 g) lean pork

½ pound (224 g) skinless and boneless chicken breast

¼ pound (112 g) unsalted pork fat

2 tablespoons butter

1 small onion, peeled and minced

½ cup (75 g) finely chopped, tart apples, such as Granny Smith

1½ teaspoons sea salt

White pepper, generous grind to taste

½ teaspoon of an equal mixture of ground cloves, ginger, coriander, and cinnamon

2 tablespoons Calvados or cognac

3 feet (.9 m) of prepared hog casing

METHOD

Par freeze the meats and fat. You will need to work quickly to keep the ingredients chilled. Have the grinder and stuffing attachments sterile and assembled. Load the casing onto the stuffing horn and set aside. Have all ingredients ready and arrayed adjacent to your work surface.

In a small sauté pan, melt the butter and cook the onion slowly until translucent. Add the apple to the pan and continue to cook for five minutes. Set aside to cool.

Slice the meats and fat into 1-inch (2.5 cm) slabs. Stack the slabs, then cut again into finger-size pieces. Grind the meat and fat together using the coarse disk for your grinder or grinder attachment.

In a large mixing bowl that has been thoroughly cleaned in soapy water and scalded with boiling water, mix the meat and fat with all remaining ingredients. Using you hands, reach across the ingredients, grasp a handful, and push it down through the center of the mass. Turn bowl a quarter turn and repeat. Continue until well mixed.

Stuff the completed forcemeat firmly into the casings. Twist the finished sausage into 3- to 6-inch (7.5 to 15 cm) links. Since you will be making links, remember to leave some slack in the casing by understuffing slightly to prevent the casing from bursting when you twist the sausage. Remove any bubbles by pricking them with a clean needle.

Since these are to be poached, it is unnecessary to dry them. Poach them for 20 minutes following the directions for poaching on page 38. The sausages are cooked after poaching. You may keep them in the refrigerator for up to three days—simply reheat to serve.

YIELD: Approximately 1½ pounds (672 g) of sausage

CERVELAS AUX PISTACHE
PISTACHIO SAUSAGE

These delicately flavored sausages are excellent breakfast food to serve with omelets. I have suggested that you poach these after stuffing them. Poaching will increase their life in the refrigerator, and they can be easily reheated. They are excellent cold with some French mustard, and look lovely sliced diagonally and arranged on a platter. The meat may be left in bulk to use as a stuffing for Cornish game hens or to make a wonderful sausage roll baked in a short crust, saucisse en croute.

INGREDIENTS

1¼ pounds (560 g) pork butt, boned and trimmed of sinew

OR,

1 pound (448 g) lean pork loin and ¼ pound (112 g) unsalted pork fat

3 ounces (85 g) shelled, unsalted pistachios, roughly chopped

1 teaspoon sea salt

Black pepper, generous grind to taste

⅛ teaspoon nutmeg

¼ teaspoon fresh thyme, or ⅛ teaspoon if using dried thyme

1 clove fresh garlic, finely minced

2 tablespoons cognac

3 feet (.9 m) of prepared hog casing

METHOD

Par freeze the meat and fat. You will need to work quickly to keep the ingredients chilled. Have the grinder and stuffing attachments sterile and assembled. Load the casing onto the stuffing horn and set aside. Have all ingredients ready and arrayed adjacent to your work surface.

Slice the meat and fat into 1-inch (2.5 cm) slabs. Stack the slabs, then cut again into finger-size pieces. Grind the meat and fat together using the coarse disk for your grinder or grinder attachment.

In a large mixing bowl that has been thoroughly cleaned in soapy water and scalded with boiling water, mix the meat and fat with all remaining ingredients. Using your hands, reach across the ingredients, grasp a handful, and push it down through the center of the mass. Turn bowl a quarter turn and repeat. Continue until well mixed.

Stuff the completed forcemeat firmly into the casings. You may leave the sausage in coils or twist the finished sausage into 3- to 4-inch (7.5 to 10 cm) links. If you will be making links, remember to leave some slack in the casing by understuffing slightly to prevent the casing from bursting when you twist the sausage. Remove any bubbles by pricking them with a clean needle.

Since these are to be poached, it is unnecessary to dry them. Poach them for 20 minutes following the directions for Poaching on page 38. The sausages are cooked after poaching. You may keep them in the refrigerator for up to three days—simply reheat to serve. Or, you can freeze the poached sausage for future use. Note: I recommend that you do not freeze these sausages, since the delicate flavor is best enjoyed soon after it is made.

YIELD:
Approximately
1½ half pounds
(672 g) of sausage

THE FRENCH WORD BOUDIN PROVIDES THE ROOT FOR THE ENGLISH WORD PUDDING. Though there is an affinity between the two words, allow me to share with you an example of how concepts often get lost in translation. I will do so by passing on a recipe for white pudding, a dish that is made throughout Great Britain in different versions. The one I share with you below has been blamed on the Scots.

WHITE PUDDING

INGREDIENTS

2 pounds (896 g) oatmeal, toasted lightly in the oven

1 pound (448 g) beef suet, finely minced

2 onions, finely minced

Salt, pepper, and sugar

METHOD

Mix all ingredients and stuff loosely in casings, tying the ends with cotton string. Boil the puddings for an hour, dry them thoroughly, and hang them in a dry ventilated space. These will keep for several months.

Or, you may throw them away immediately. Yes, I understand that these may be appealing to some, just not to me.

I suppose that I should apologize for this cultural slur. I actually have an abiding love for Scotland. Having completed my military obligation in the late 1960s almost unscathed but with a small pension, I scooted across the pond and fetched up on the Scottish Isle of Arran. I intended to spend a month there finding myself; instead, I stayed for two years among the sweetest people I have ever known.

Still, as much as I love Scotland, I ate more turnips with cheese sauce than a man should. It is true that my budget forced me into a diet even more bland than was customary. I still shudder when I think of the Burns' Night Supper I attended. These yearly feasts revolve around a meal that is possible only in a land that has produced single malt whiskey. The whiskey, you see, is so ambrosial and powerful, that when you are under its influence you can eat anything.

The traditional menu on these evenings included Haggis, boiled turnips, boiled potatoes, and boiled suet pudding. Haggis, if you don't already know, is a dish consisting of a mixture of the minced heart, lungs, and liver of a sheep or calf mixed with suet, onions, oatmeal, and seasonings, and boiled in the stomach of the slaughtered animal. In order to convince us to eat the Haggis, we were not only plied with malt whiskey but serenaded with Burns' poetry, climaxing with his immortal *Address to a Haggis*.

While I have not been kidding about the previous British dishes, I will continue by saying that Great Britain has a more conventional, and quite delicious, sausage larder. The British idiosyncrasy is to rely on grain and bread extenders, providing results that are actually very good. The bangers and oyster sausage that follow are two that I have enjoyed.

British bangers and mash (mashed potatoes) are pub food staples.

ADDRESS TO A HAGGIS

– I –

Fair fa' your honest, sonsie face,
Great chieftain o' the puddin-race!
Aboon them a' ye tak your place,
    Painch, tripe, or thairm;
Weel are ye wordy of a grace
    As lang's my arm

– II –

The groaning trencher there ye fill,
Your hurdies like a distant hill,
Your pin wad help to mend a mill
    In time o' need,
While thro' your pores the dews distil
    Like amber bead...

– V –

Os there that owre his French ragout
or olio that wad staw a sow
Or fricasse wad mak her spew
    Wi perfect sconner,
Looks down, wi sneering, scoenful view
    On sic a dinner?...

– VII –

But mark the Rustic, haggis-fed,
The trembling earth resounds his tread,
Clap in his wailie nieve a blade,
    He'll make it whissle;
An' legs, an' arms, an heads will sned
    Like taps of' thrissle.

– VIII –

Ye Pow'rs wha make mankind your care,
And dish them out their bill o' fare,
Auld Scotland wants nae skinking ware,
    That jaups in luggies;
But, if ye wish her gratefu' prayer
    Gie her a Haggis!

BANGERS

Bangers (or Oxford sausages) are perhaps the best known and most common of British sausage. I have maintained the traditional percentage of fat for these versatile treats, although you may wish to reduce it somewhat. Be mindful that the bread will tend to dry out the sausages if you use too little fat.

INGREDIENTS

- ½ pound (224 g) of lean pork
- ½ pound (224 g) of lean veal
- ½ pound (224 g) unsalted pork fat
- 3 slices white bread with crust, finely chopped
- 1 cup (240 mL) heavy cream
- 1 teaspoon sea salt
- ¼ teaspoon black pepper
- ¼ teaspoon cayenne
- ⅛ teaspoon of an equal mixture of ground nutmeg and mace
- ⅛ teaspoon each of crumbled thyme and marjoram
- 1 teaspoon crumbled sage
- 1 teaspoon finely grated lemon peel
- 1 large whole egg
- 3 feet (.9 m) of prepared hog casing

METHOD

Par freeze the meats and fat. Have the grinder and stuffing attachments sterile and assembled. Load the casing onto the stuffing horn and set aside. Have all ingredients ready and arrayed adjacent to your work surface.

Slice the meats and fat into 1-inch (2.5 cm) slabs. Stack the slabs, then cut again into finger-size pieces. Grind the meat and fat together using the coarse disk for your grinder or grinder attachment.

In a large mixing bowl that has been thoroughly cleaned in soapy water and scalded with boiling water, knead the meats, fat, and bread together until well mixed. Add the remaining ingredients and mix. Using your hands, reach across the ingredients to grasp a handful, and push it down through the center of the mass. Turn bowl a quarter turn and repeat. Continue until well mixed.

Stuff the completed forcemeat firmly into the casings. Twist the finished sausage into 4- to 6-inch (10 to 15 cm) links. Since you will be making links, remember to leave some slack in the casing by understuffing slightly to prevent the casing from bursting when you twist the sausage. Remove any bubbles by pricking them with a clean needle.

If you will be cooking the sausage within three days, arrange on sheet pans and refrigerate, uncovered, overnight to dry the skins. Then cook, or wrap and store the sausages in the refrigerator until ready to cook. Freeze the remainder of the sausage in meal-sized portions by first wrapping the portions in butcher or wax paper, then placing the wrapped portion in freezer bags from which you remove as much air as possible.

When you wish to defrost sausage, place the package in the refrigerator overnight before unwrapping.

YIELD: Approximately 2 pounds (896 g) of sausage

OYSTER SAUSAGE

These are very simple bulk sausages, coming from a time when oysters were far cheaper than meat in both England and America. Today they make an exotic main course. You can also cook and drain the sausage patties, then break them up into a cornbread stuffing or add the crumbled sausage to a soup.

INGREDIENTS

- 2 cups (448 g) chopped raw oysters
- 1 pound (448 g) lean veal
- 1 slice bacon
- ½ cup (70 g) bread crumbs
- 2 teaspoons sea salt
- 1 teaspoon white pepper
- ¼ teaspoon nutmeg
- Butter, enough for frying the sausage

METHOD

Using a food processor with the steel blade, emulsify the oysters, veal, and bacon.

Place the emulsified ingredients in a bowl. Add the bread crumbs, salt, pepper, and nutmeg. Using a spoon, mix the ingredients together. The mixture will be sticky, so moisten your hands and form them into four to six patties, each approximately ½ inch (1.3 cm) thick.

To cook, heat the butter in a skillet and brown the patties all over. When browned, add enough water to the pan to come halfway up the sides of the sausages. Reduce the heat to medium low, cover and simmer for 8 minutes until the patties are cooked through.

YIELD: 4–6 patties

stocks and broths: *pot-au-feu*

Recognizing that I tend to the extreme in the world of cooking and food, I still believe there are some traditional procedures that clearly make all the difference. If I were reduced to espousing one principle alone, it would be that food benefits more from decent stocks than any other single element. Most people avoid making their own stocks because they view it as a labor of intensive drudgery. Not so.

The liquid by-product of poaching a chicken, fish, or vegetables will make an easy, mild, but serviceable stock. For a full-bodied stock, get in the habit of saving the liquid whenever you poach, then freeze it, and use it the next time you poach something. Continue this process as many times as desired. In this way, you gradually achieve the enriching broth of a pot-au-feu, or fire pot, meaning pot on the stove. In the ideal French farmhouse, this wonderful dish is simply the accumulation of scraps of meat and herbs that is kept bubbling on the back of the stove.

Over time, you'll find that you have created a true, rich stock that will fill the house with warm, delectable aromas—enough to fool anyone who walks in. Only you will know how simple the process is, and how little stove time it actually involves.

THOUGH THERE IS A DARKNESS AND MYSTERY TO THE FOODS OF ALL SPANISH-SPEAKING COUNTRIES, THOSE OF US WHO HAVE SAMPLED THE AUTHENTIC CUISINES HAVE BEEN WON OVER. However, with the exception of a hybrid Mexican cuisine, restaurants that represent the savory and spicy spectrum of these cooking traditions are rare in the United States. Fortunately this is changing, particularly in large cities.

There have always been many wonderful Hispanic/Portuguese restaurants in those cities fortunate to have strong expatriate communities. In Miami, one can eat Cuban foods; in Providence, Rhode Island, Portuguese; in Honolulu, Hawaii, Philippine; and in Washington, D.C., Salvadoran, Colombian, and Brazilian delicacies. (Note that I group the cuisine under the heading Hispanic/Portuguese as a convenience only; the variety of foods from Spain, Portugal, Mexico, the many countries of Latin America and the Caribbean, parts of Africa, and the Philippines is wildly disparate.)

Until recently, a fast-food chain was the only connection most of us have had to the foods of the Iberian peninsula and its former colonies around the world. While the hybrids Tex-Mex, New Mex-Mex, and California-Mex are each interesting and often very satisfying cuisines, they are, frankly, very different from the authentic (and multiple) cuisines of Mexico. I said earlier in the section on Italy, "…if I *had to choose* one and only one culinary source, I would not hesitate to choose Italy." Let me add that the cuisine I might miss most if I did make such a choice would be Mexican.

Very much like the Italian approach to foods, fresh ingredients at the peak of their flavor are crucial to Mexican food. I recommend that you travel within Mexico to sample the enormous fiesta that is celebrated at their national dining table. One reason that I make this suggestion is the labor-intensiveness of Mexican cooking. A close friend who traveled widely in Latin America, and who shared my love for these foods, once said to me as we happily waded through elaborate dishes, "The secret to Mexican cooking is to begin with servants."

The fact that this book interests you, however, suggests that you, like me and my friends, are willing to go the extra mile in the kitchen. Therefore, I recommend for further study all of the wonderful books written by the doyen (for the English-speaking world) of Mexican cuisines, Diana Kennedy.

My concentration on Mexico (and the Mexican approach to chorizo sausage that follows) is simply because of my personal experience and infatuation with that country's food. Equal rhapsody is due to Spain, Portugal, and, in fact, each of those Latin countries blessed with rich soil or waters to create and sustain the traditions of great food. Following you will find three recipes for wonderful sausage—one each from Mexico, Spain, and Portugal.

Caldo verde, flavored with kale, potatoes, and chorizo, is quick and easy to make. (recipe on page 96)

LINGUIÇA

Linguiça is an important component of Portuguese cuisine and is most often smoked. The Spanish equivalent, longaniza, is most often made and used fresh. This version is a compromise and suggests liquid smoke (unless you have access to a smoker). Either way, this sausage benefits from a two- to three-day refrigeration period before cooking (or smoking) to develop the flavors.

INGREDIENTS

1¼ pounds (560 g) pork butt
OR,

1 pound (448 g) lean pork and ¼ pound (112 g) unsalted pork fat

1½ teaspoons sea salt

2 teaspoons sweet paprika

1 teaspoon fresh rosemary, finely minced

2 cloves of fresh garlic, finely minced

2 tablespoons of white vinegar

½ teaspoon liquid smoke (omit if you will be smoking these)

3 feet (.9 m) of prepared hog casing

METHOD

Par freeze the meat and fat. Have the grinder and stuffing attachments sterile and assembled. Load the casing onto the stuffing horn and set aside. Have all ingredients ready and arrayed adjacent to your work surface.

Slice the meat and fat into 1-inch (2.5 cm) slabs. Stack the slabs, then cut again into finger-size pieces. Grind the meat and fat together using the coarse disk for your grinder or grinder attachment.

In a large mixing bowl that has been thoroughly cleaned in soapy water and scalded with boiling water, mix the meat and fat with all remaining ingredients. Using your hands, reach across the ingredients, grasp a handful, and push it down through the center of the mass. Turn bowl a quarter turn and repeat. Continue until well mixed.

Stuff the completed forcemeat firmly into the casings. You may leave the sausage in coils or twist the finished sausage into 3- to 6-inch (7.5 to 15 cm) links. If you will be making links, remember to leave some slack in the casing by understuffing slightly to prevent the casing from bursting when you twist the sausage. Pierce any air pockets with a clean needle.

To develop the flavor before cooking, place the sausage in a colander, loosely covering (not wrapping) the sausage with wax paper or plastic wrap. Place the colander over a pan that is large enough to catch the drippings and place in the refrigerator for two to three days. Discard the drippings daily. Then cook, or wrap and store the sausages in the refrigerator until ready to cook. Use within three days. You may also smoke the sausages after developing the flavor. (See page 39 for general directions for smoking, or follow the manufacturer's instructions for your smoker.)

YIELD: Approximately 1½ pounds (672 kg) of sausage

BUTIFARRA

This delicious sausage comes from Catalonia in northeast Spain. The spicing is complex, and while it is excellent in casseroles or stews, it shines in clear soups. The Spanish institution of tapas, or light meals composed of small portions of several appetizers, features omelets cut into small pieces and served with toast. The Spanish omelet is called a tortilla, and the tortilla Gallego features sausage and potato—butifarra serves this dish superbly.

INGREDIENTS

2 pounds (896 g) pork butt

OR,

1½ pounds (672 g) lean pork and ½ pound (224 g) unsalted pork fat

2 tablespoons white wine

⅛ teaspoon each, cinnamon, nutmeg, cloves, and thyme

2 teaspoons sea salt

⅛ teaspoon sweet paprika

¼ teaspoon black pepper, ground

3 feet (.9 m) of prepared hog casing

METHOD

Par freeze the meat and fat. Have the grinder and stuffing attachments sterile and assembled. Load the casing onto the stuffing horn and set aside. Have all ingredients ready and arrayed adjacent to your work surface.

Slice the meat and fat into 1-inch (2.5 cm) slabs. Stack the slabs, then cut again into finger-size pieces. Grind the meat and fat together using the coarse disk for your grinder or grinder attachment.

Mix the wine with the herbs and spices before mixing with the meat and fat. Put all ingredients in a large mixing bowl that has been thoroughly cleaned in soapy water and scalded with boiling water. Using your hands, reach across the ingredients, grasp a handful, and push it down through the center of the mass. Turn bowl a quarter turn and repeat. Continue until well mixed.

Stuff the completed forcemeat firmly into the casings to form two 30-inch (75 cm) links. Remove any air pockets by piercing them with a clean needle.

Arrange the sausages on a sheet pan and refrigerate, uncovered, for two days to dry the skins. After two days, poach the sausages (see page 38) for 40 minutes. To serve, reheat, or cool and wrap the sausages to store in the refrigerator or freeze.

YIELD: Approximately 2 pounds (896 g) of sausage

round-and-round

Ring bologna and other sausages with ring-like or round shapes that you find in the grocery store are most likely encased in beef rounds. They are the part of the intestine that naturally forms a spiral, making them the perfect choice for encasing recipes that call for this traditional shaping.

CHORIZO

It is probable that every Spanish-speaking country has multiple versions of this sausage. They all contain pork, spices, and vinegar, but beyond that, the variations are many. I am particularly fond of this version to which I have added chipotle peppers—the smoked and dried jalapeños with a very special kick. This recipe is quite spicy, and you may wish to substitute a mild chile powder for the chile mixture.

INGREDIENTS

2½ pounds (1.12 kg) pork butt

OR,

2 pounds (896 g) of lean pork and ½ pound (224 g) unsalted pork fat

5 chiles anchos, minced

2 dried chiles chipotle (or 2 chiles in adobo sauce), minced

½ teaspoon ground coriander

3 whole cloves, ground fresh

½ teaspoon peppercorns

½ teaspoon oregano

¼ teaspoon cumin seed

2 tablespoons sweet paprika

4 cloves fresh garlic, minced

2½ teaspoons sea salt

⅓ cup (80 mL) white vinegar

4 feet (1.2 m) of prepared hog casing

NOTE: Chorizo are often skinned, crumbled, fried, and drained before being added to dishes.

YIELD: Approximately 2½ pounds (1.12 kg) of sausage

METHOD

Par freeze the meat and fat. Have the grinder and stuffing attachments sterile and assembled. Load the casing onto the stuffing horn and set aside. Have all ingredients ready and arrayed adjacent to your work surface.

Place all the dried spices, including chiles, in a dry frying pan and heat until ingredients are pungent and toasted but not smoking. Place them in a coffee grinder, spice mill, or mortar and grind. Set aside.

Slice the meat and fat into 1-inch (2.5 cm) slabs. Stack the slabs, then cut again into finger-size pieces. Grind the meat and fat together using the coarse disk for your grinder or grinder attachment.

In a large mixing bowl that has been thoroughly cleaned in soapy water and scalded with boiling water, mix the meat and fat with all remaining ingredients. Using your hands, reach across the ingredients, grasp a handful, and push it down through the center of the mass. Turn bowl a quarter turn and repeat. Continue until well mixed.

Stuff the completed forcemeat firmly into the casings. You may leave the sausage in coils or twist the finished sausage into 3- to 6-inch (7.5 to 15 cm) links. If you will be making links, remember to leave some slack in the casing by understuffing slightly to prevent the casing from bursting when you twist the sausage. Pierce any air pockets with a clean needle.

These sausages taste better and will keep longer in the refrigerator or freezer if they are slightly dried. To do this, place the fresh sausages in a colander, loosely covering (not wrapping) the sausage with wax paper or plastic wrap. Place the colander over a pan that is large enough to catch the drippings, and place in the refrigerator. The sausages will drain liquid for up to three days. Discard the liquid daily. After three days, arrange the sausage on a sheet pan, making sure you separate them from each other. Bake at 200°F (95°C) for 5 hours. Allow to cool, then wrap and store them in the refrigerator for up to two weeks, or you can store them for many months in the freezer

making seafood sausage

In my experimentation with seafood sausage, I have made some with great success. From my experience, I want to encourage an adventurous spirit—with some warnings. First, keep in mind that most seafood flavors and textures are ephemeral, requiring that seafood be cooked to just the right degree. If you overcook, you bleach the flavor and toughen the texture. If you over-spice, you overwhelm the delicate flavor.

Confusingly, there are exceptions to both rules. Shrimp, crab, and clams can withstand high spice and still exert their flavors. Octopus and squid need lengthy cooking, except when small young specimens are available.

Unlike red meats and poultry, seafood, when ground, cannot be easily formed into shapes. Seafood has a very high moisture content and relatively low viscosity (a kind of well-behaved stickiness) which make it hard to work with. Furthermore, seafood tends to be very low in fat content.

To give seafood sausage some body, grind the seafood with some bread, cooked rice, or potato, then mix with beaten egg. You can also emulsify the seafood in the food processor, adding the binding ingredients toward the end of the process. Another approach is to leave some of the seafood in pieces to mix with ground or emulsified ingredients, providing a visual and textural mosaic to the finished sausage.

The preferred (and my recommended) method for cooking seafood sausage is to poach it gently and briefly until warm. This allows the juices to remain in the seafood both to enhance the flavor and keep the delicate texture. Once the sausages are poached you can eat them immediately. Or, as the French do, let them cool, cut the casings away, roll the sausages gently in fine bread crumbs, then sauté lightly in butter and serve. Bon appétit!

ABOVE: You can handstuff the emulsified seafood forcemeat.

BELOW: To poach, place sausage in the hot water.

SEAFOOD SAUSAGE

I was raised in a seagoing family. My parents both joined the Coast Guard at the outbreak of World War II. Mother was one of the original SPARS, and the two of them became the first American military officer couple to be married. Dad made a career of it, so for the first 18 years of my life, I was never further than a few miles from the sea.

As a 13 year old, I spent nine months on the Basswood, a buoy tender out of Honolulu. We sailed from our home port to Yokusuka, Japan. I ate some of almost everything that came from the ocean, raw and cooked, from giant clam chowder at an island called Falalop in the Ulithi atoll of Micronesia, to sashimi of tuna belly in Tokyo. If I was ever indifferent to seafood, I cannot remember it.

When it came to this book, I looked forward to making seafood sausage—and I have not been disappointed! Here is a base recipe for which you can substitute any fresh fish or shellfish. Look for clear-eyed fish and sweet-smelling bivalves. The good stuff should not smell fishy at all. While I recognize the contradiction, I do find frozen seafood to be acceptable *if and only if* I can't get fresh. I think of frozen seafood almost as a different food to which I bring different expectations.

I like to poach my seafood sausage in a fish or mixed fish and shellfish fumet, which is a concentrated stock. If I don't have available stock, I will, in a pinch, use bottled clam juice and water in a ratio of 1 to 1. For this recipe (and any that contain raw egg) stuff loosely, since the egg will expand as it cooks.

Even out the seafood forcemeat in the casing by running your hand over the sausage two or three times.

Twist the sausage into links

Use short lengths of kitchen twine to tie off the twists.

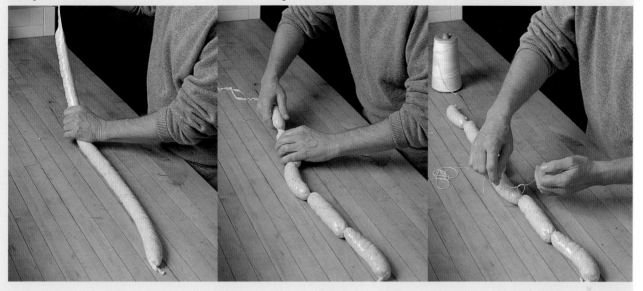

INGREDIENTS

1 pound (448 g) fish fillet (choose a mild, non-oily ocean fish such as flounder, cod, or salmon), cubed

¼ pound (112 g) bay scallops

¼ pound (112 g) crab meat, picked over to remove cartilage

¼ pound (112 g) shucked oysters (optional)

½ pound (224 g) small shrimp, peeled and deveined

½ teaspoon sea salt

¼ cup (45 g) onion, minced

2 eggs, lightly beaten

1 teaspoon fresh dill, minced (½ teaspoon if using dried)

2 cloves fresh garlic, minced

¼ cup (60 mL) heavy cream

½ cup (65 g) unseasoned bread crumbs (optional)

3 feet (.9 m) of prepared hog casing.

METHOD

Have the stuffing equipment sterile and assembled. Load the casing onto the stuffing horn and set aside. Have the food processor assembled. Have all ingredients ready and arrayed adjacent to your work surface.

Using the food processor with the steel blade, process all ingredients until emulsified. The forcemeat will resemble a fine, moist paste. If the mixture is too moist, you may wish to add some or all of the bread crumbs to stiffen the mixture before stuffing.

Stuff the forcemeat loosely (since the egg will expand) into the prepared casings. Since the forcemeat is so moist, run your hand over the sausage once or twice after it is stuffed to smooth and even out the forcemeat in the casing. Twist into 7-inch (17.5 cm) links, using kitchen twine to tie off between the links. Remove any air pockets by piercing them with a clean needle.

Poach the sausage for 20 minutes (see the directions for Poaching on page 38). Serve immediately or within 24 hours. You may also wrap and freeze them, where they will keep for three months. To serve, gently reheat by poaching in a flavored broth or dry white wine and water in a ratio of 1 to 1. Or, remove the casings by gently cutting them away, dip the sausage in beaten egg, roll in bread crumbs, and fry in butter until golden.

YIELD: Approximately 3 pounds (1.36 kg) of sausage

THERE ARE IDIOSYNCRATIC APPROACHES TO MEALS THAT OFTEN MAKE IT EASY TO IDENTIFY THE COUNTRY BY THE TABLE. As you might expect, the preservation of foods would be an important consideration for countries with limited growing and hunting seasons. While the requirements of the land shape a cuisine, the foods and food traditions that are subsequently produced define the country. The countries of Scandinavia are renowned (at least in Europe) for their preserved meats. While there are very interesting differences between each country's approach, one of the shared characteristics is unusual spicing such as ginger and cardamom. Norwegian sausages, called pølse (as they are also known in Denmark), tend to rely on herbs for flavoring, while the others tend toward spices.

While lamb is rare in Denmark and in Sweden, it is prized in Norway. Danish sausages benefit from the extremely high standards that the country assigns to its beef and pork. Blood sausages in many forms have always been popular and continue so in Norway. Reindeer meat, all but unheard of in the rest of the world, is exported from Lapland to all of Scandinavia.

The sausage (as well as the entire cuisine) of Finland is influenced by its disparate neighbors, Sweden and Russia. Finnish sausage, makkara, and other meats were once grilled on the stones that provide the heat in saunas. Today, it is common for sauna dressing rooms to have fireplaces for this purpose. Scandinavians prefer a thick yellow pea soup with chunks of smoked sausage, while further south in Belgium, the same dish is served with green split peas.

I have included a recipe for Swedish potato sausage julkorv (*korv* is the Swedish word for sausage) that is central to their Christmas table. These treats are part of the elaborate set of customs and rituals that revolve around this important holiday. I once enjoyed a Christmas with a Swedish-American family that seemed to share dozens of events and meals that were clearly annual expectations. I particularly enjoyed a wonderful braided bread flavored with dill weed. After the holiday, I asked the hostess to make it again. She was astounded that I might even consider eating this Christmas dish out of its season!

To extend the life of the meats, the Swedes often store them in a sugar and salt brine. This instinct to store and preserve for the winter is carried by the Swedes throughout the world. I had a shipmate on an ocean-going towboat where I cooked for a summer who traveled everywhere with an oak cask and pickling spices. He often put up herring, but it could have easily been värmlandskorv, a variation on the following recipe for Christmas sausage.

Split pea soup and julkorv, a potatoe sausage, is classic Scandinavian fare. (recipe for soup is on page 110)

INGREDIENTS

1 pound (448 g) lean pork, finely ground

1 pound (448 g) lean beef, finely ground

½ pound (224 g) unsalted pork fat

1 cup (240 mL) milk

½ teaspoon ground allspice

¼ teaspoon crumbled marjoram

⅛ teaspoon thyme

1 teaspoon ground black pepper

2 teaspoons sea salt

1 tablespoon sugar

1 pound (448 g) of potatoes, peeled and grated

4 teaspoons coarse salt

2 teaspoons sugar

4 feet (1.2 m) of prepared hog casing

YIELD: Approximately 3 pounds (1.36 kg) of sausage

JULKORV
CHRISTMAS POTATO SAUSAGE

Potatoes form the center of much of the world's cuisines, and nowhere more than throughout Scandinavia. Each country has its own version of potato sausage, both in everyday varieties and those reserved exclusively for the Christmas season. This Swedish form includes allspice with some sugar, producing the typical northern characteristic of sausage flavored with spice. These sausages can either be enjoyed poached or poached first, then browned.

METHOD

Par freeze the meats and fat. Have the grinder and stuffing attachments sterile and assembled. Load the casing onto the stuffing horn and set aside. Have all ingredients ready and arrayed adjacent to your work surface.

Slice the meats and fat into 1-inch (2.5 cm) slabs. Stack the slabs, then cut again into finger-size pieces. Grind the meats together using the fine disk for your grinder or grinder attachment.

To the milk, add the allspice, marjoram, thyme, black pepper, the 2 teaspoons of sea salt, and the tablespoon of sugar. In a large mixing bowl that has been thoroughly cleaned in soapy water and scalded with boiling water, use your hands to mix the ground beef and pork with the potatoes. When well mixed, add the milk and spice mixture to the meat and potatoes. Use a wooden spoon to beat together until fluffy. (I prefer using the paddle attachment with my electric mixer.)

Stuff the completed forcemeat firmly into the casings. You can either form 6-inch (15 cm) links, or much longer ones that are 18 to 24 inches (45.5 to 61 cm) long. Since you will be making links, remember to leave some slack in the casing by understuffing slightly to prevent the casing from bursting when you twist the sausage. Remove any air pockets by piercing them with a clean needle. Mix the remaining sugar with the coarse salt, and rub over the sausages.

Place the sasuage in a covered bowl and place in the refrigerator. Keep in this way until the sausages no longer release liquid; this can take up to two days. Rinse the sausage.

Poach the sausages for 30 minutes (see the directions for Poaching on page 38). At this point the sausages are ready to eat, or you can brown them in a skillet before serving. You can also cool the sausages after poaching, then wrap and store them in the refrigerator for up to five days.

INGEFARAPOLSE

This Norwegian bulk sausage makes delightful meatballs. This variation on the preceding Swedish potato sausage features ginger and an additional surprise that works—chopped sour pickle.

INGREDIENTS

- 1 pound (448 g) of julkorv forcemeat
- 3 tablespoons onion, minced
- ¾ teaspoon ginger, ground
- ⅛ teaspoon cloves, ground
- ⅛ teaspoon white pepper
- ⅛ teaspoon sea salt
- 2 egg whites from large eggs
- 1 tablespoon cornichon (or other sour pickle), minced
- ¼ cup (25 g) dry bread crumbs
- Vegetable oil

METHOD

Prepare the julkorv forcemeat following the directions on page 70. To this, add the onion. Remember to beat the mixture with a wooden spoon (or paddle attachment on the electric mixer) until fluffy.

In a separate bowl mix the ginger, cloves, pepper, salt, and egg whites. Whip until the egg whites hold stiff peaks. Fold the egg mixture gently into the sausage meat, then fold in the pickles and bread crumbs.

Form the mixture into balls that are approximately 1½ inches (4 cm) in diameter. Moisten your hands before handling, since the mixture will be sticky. Heat the oil in a skillet, and thoroughly brown the meatballs all over.

YEILD: Approximately 12 meatballs

master batching

Take advantage of particularly good buys in meats and seafood to buy in quantity for creating handy master batches. Grind large amounts of meat and fat either separately or in a ratio of 4 to 1. Portion the mixtures into logical amounts such as 1 pound (.5 kg) meat packages and 1/4 pound (112 g) fat packages and freeze. If you find a sausage recipe that you are particularly fond of, grind large quantities of meat and mix in the ingredients as directed, then freeze the force-meat for future stuffing.

taste testing

Unlike working with other recipes and ingredients, taste testing a sausage mixture is not as easy as licking the spoon or dipping a finger in the batter. Since you're working with raw meat, you will need to cook the meat before testing. To do this, always keep a small frying pan handy. When you have completed mixing the recipe, take a small bit of the meat mixture and make a small patty. Fry the patty until done, then taste. Adjust the seasoning accordingly before you stuff the sausage into the casing.

MEDVURST

This is a traditional smoked beef and pork sausage that is delicious in vegetable or pea soups. In Denmark, beautiful open-faced sandwiches called smørrebrød are often topped with poached slices of this sausage. If you come from the northern Midwest of the United States and remember smorgasbord, you may have tasted this sausage.

INGREDIENTS

1 pound (448 g) lean pork, finely ground

1 pound (448 g) lean beef, finely ground

¼ pound (112 g) unsalted pork fat, finely ground

¼ cup (60 mL) lager beer

2 teaspoons sea salt

1 teaspoon sugar

½ teaspoon ground black pepper

⅛ teaspoon ground cloves

⅛ teaspoon nutmeg

¼ teaspoon caraway seeds

¼ teaspoon ground coriander

⅜ teaspoon dried mustard

½ teaspoon liquid smoke (omit if you will be smoking these)

4 teaspoons coarse salt

2 teaspoons sugar

4 feet (1.2 m) of prepared hog casing

METHOD

Par freeze the meats and fat. Have the grinder and stuffing attachments sterile and assembled. Load the casing onto the stuffing horn and set aside. Have all ingredients ready and arrayed adjacent to your work surface.

Slice the meats and fat into 1-inch (2.5 cm) slabs. Stack the slabs, then cut again into finger-size pieces. Grind the meats and fat together using the fine disk for your grinder or grinder attachment.

Add all but the 4 teaspoons of coarse salt and 2 teaspoons of sugar to the beer. In a large mixing bowl that has been thoroughly cleaned in soapy water and scalded with boiling water, use your hands to mix the ground beef, pork, and fat together. When well mixed, add the beer mixture to the meat.

Stuff the completed forcemeat firmly into the casings. Twist into 4-inch (10 cm) links. Since you will be making links, remember to leave some slack in the casing by understuffing slightly to prevent the casing from bursting when you twist the sausage. Remove any air pockets by piercing them with a clean needle. Mix the remaining sugar with the coarse salt and rub over the sausages.

Place the sausages in a colander, loosely covering (not wrapping) the sausage with wax paper or plastic wrap. Place the colander over a pan that is large enough to catch the drippings, and place in the refrigerator. Keep in this way until the sausages no longer release liquid. This can take up to two days. Rinse the sausages.

Poach the sausages for 20 minutes (see the directions for Poaching on page 38). Alternatively if you have a smoker, rinse and wipe the sausages after they have finished releasing liquid. Smoke them at 275˚F (135˚C) until they reach an internal temperature of 170˚F (77˚C). This should take approximately 4 hours. (See the basic directions for smoking on page 39.)

YIELD: Approximately 2½ pounds (1.12 kg) of sausage

KAALIKAARYLEET

Have you considered that stuffed cabbage meets most of the definition of sausage? You can also use grape leaves, onions, or lettuce leaves as your casing. Some historians have speculated that the Vikings, who traded with Constantinople in the 10th century, might have brought back from the Middle East the notion of forcemeat stuffed into vegetables. Here is a Finnish version that contains barley.

INGREDIENTS

- ⅓ cup (67 g) pearl barley, soaked in water to cover for 1 to 4 hours
- 1 cup (240 mL) water
- 1 large head of cabbage
- 1 pound (448 g) beef with approximately 20% fat, coarsely ground ¼ pound (112 g) veal, coarsely ground
- 1 teaspoon sea salt
- ¼ teaspoon black pepper
- ½ teaspoon allspice
- ¼ cup (60 mL) heavy cream
- 3 tablespoons unsalted butter
- 4 teaspoons molasses
- 1 tablespoon white flour

YIELD: Approximately 12 rolls

METHOD

Drain the barley and cook in the water for 30 minutes. Strain and cool. Boil the cabbage in a large pot of water for 10 minutes, or until the leaves are pliable.

If you are grinding your own meat, par freeze the meat, then slice into 1-inch (2.5 cm) slabs. Stack the slabs, then cut again into finger-size pieces. Grind the meats together using the coarse disk for your grinder or grinder attachment.

Put the barley, meats, salt, pepper, allspice, and cream in a large mixing bowl that has been thoroughly cleaned in soapy water and scalded with boiling water. Mix by hand until well mixed.

Carefully detach 12 large cabbage leaves and cut out the hard rib of the stem, allowing the leaves to fold without breaking.

Place a generous tablespoonful of the filling on the leaf, leaving a 1-inch (2.5 cm) border on each side of the leaf, and a ½-inch (1.5 cm) border on the end nearest to you. Fold the sides over the meat toward the center, then roll the package up away from you. Repeat until the filling is gone.

Preheat the oven to 350˚F (175˚C). Melt the butter in an ovenproof skillet large enough to contain all of the cabbage rolls. Place the rolls in the skillet, seam side down, and brown on all sides, turning as needed. Carefully pour in enough water to not quite cover the rolls, and place in the oven for 1 hour. Drizzle the molasses over the rolls, and bake an additional 30 minutes.

Remove the rolls from the skillet, keeping them covered and warm. Place the skillet on the stove top. Over medium heat, gradually stir in the flour and cook, stirring until the sauce is smooth and thickend. Pour over the rolls and serve.

RIISMAKKARA

This Finnish sausage provides a lovely contrast in flavors and textures between rice, raisins, and the richness of liver. These can be served as chilled slices for an appetizer, or skinned and mixed with cream cheese as a spread. When making the sausage, try to avoid breaking up the rice and raisins; maintaining the contrast in textures is an important part of this recipe.

INGREDIENTS

- 2¼ cups (540 mL) milk
- ½ cup (112 g) rice
- ½ pound (224 g) beef or pork liver, finely ground
- 1 small onion, minced
- 3 tablespoons unsalted butter (or beef suet)
- 3 tablespoons corn syrup
- ½ teaspoon ginger
- 6 tablespoons raisins
- 1 teaspoon salt
- ¼ teaspoon black pepper
- 2 feet (.6 m) of prepared hog casing

METHOD

Have the grinder and stuffing attachments sterile and assembled. Load the casing onto the stuffing horn and set aside. Have all ingredients ready and arrayed adjacent to your work surface.

Bring 1½ cups (360 mL) of the milk to a boil. Add the rice, and lower the heat to a low simmer. Cover and cook for 15 minutes or until the milk has been absorbed. Be careful that the rice does not burn. Cool.

If you are grinding your own liver, par freeze the liver, then slice into 1-inch (2.5 cm) slabs. Stack the slabs, then cut again into finger-size pieces. Grind the liver using the fine disk for your grinder or grinder attachment.

Melt the butter or suet slowly in a skillet, then cook the onion in it until it is translucent. Add the liver and break it up as small as you can while it cooks. Remove from the heat, and cool slightly.

In a large bowl, add the contents of the skillet, the rice, and the remaining ingredients, including the rest of the milk. Stuff the completed forcemeat loosely into the casings. Twist the sausage into 4-inch (10 cm) links, using kitchen twine to tie off between the links. Remove any air pockets by piercing them with a clean needle.

Poach the sausage for 45 minutes. (See the directions for Poaching on page 38.) If the sausage floats during poaching, prick them a few times with a fork. After poaching, the sausages are ready to eat. Or, wrap and refrigerate for use within five days. These sausages do not freeze well.

YIELD: Approximately 1¼ pounds (560 g) of sausage

making game sausage

If you hunt, or know someone who does, you'll find that making (and eating) sausage from game will provide you with one of the world's tastiest offerings. Handling game meat when making sausage follows the basic procedures of grinding, mixing, and stuffing. However, since game meat tends to be lean, be aware that you may need to add additional fat in the form of suet or fatback to reach the ideal 20 to 25 percent fat to lean ratio. You can judge this by examining the cut of meat for the amount of marbling running through the flesh. Also be aware that game may need more attention when trimming tendons and sinew from the meat. Some traditional seasonings you may want to try in your game sausage are sage and garlic. If you want to experiment further, try dried mushrooms (that have been soaked) and walnuts in the recipe for an earthy complement.

GAME SAUSAGE

As discussed, the original purpose of sausage was to make the best use of meats when slaughtering took place. It is rare for us today to need to preserve a full carcass except, of course, when hunting season is on. Venison, rabbit, duck, boar... all wild game, is excellent for sausage. The following recipe comes from a restaurant in San Antonio, Texas, that specializes in southwestern cuisine. If you do not have a good source for fresh rattlesnake meat, venison will do.

INGREDIENTS

- ½ pound (224 g) rattlesnake meat
- ¼ pound (112 g) lean pork
- ¼ pound (112 g) fatback, blanched and drained
- 1 tablespoon brandy
- 2 teaspoons cumin, ground
- 1 teaspoon salt
- 1 teaspoon white pepper, ground
- ½ teaspoon smoked venison (you can substitute Canadian bacon), diced
- 1 tablespoon fresh tarragon (or 1 teaspoon if using dried)
- 2 tablespoons red pepper, diced
- 2 feet (.6 m) of prepared hog casing

METHOD

Bone and skin the rattlesnake.

Par freeze the meat and fat. Have the grinder and stuffing attachments sterile and assembled. Load the casing onto the stuffing horn and set aside. Have all ingredients ready and arrayed adjacent to your work surface.

Slice the meat and fat into 1-inch (2.5 cm) slabs. Stack the slabs, then cut again into finger-size pieces. Grind the meat and fat together using the coarse disk for your grinder or grinder attachment.

In a food processor with a steel blade, mix the spices and brandy with the ground meat and fat. Process until the mixture resembles a fine paste. In a large mixing bowl that has been thoroughly cleaned in soapy water and scalded with boiling water, mix the meat mixture with the diced smoked meat, tarragon, and red pepper.

Stuff the completed forcemeat firmly into the casings. Twist the sausage into 4- to 6- inch (10 to 15 cm) links. Since you will be making links, remember to leave some slack in the casing by understuffing slightly to prevent the casing from bursting when you twist the sausage. Remove any air pockets by piercing them with a sterile needle.

Poach the sausage for 30 minutes (see the directions for Poaching on page 38). Eat immediately by preparing as desired (they are also very good smoked). Or cool, wrap, and store in the refrigerator for five days or in the freezer for three months.

YIELD: Approximately 1 pound (448 g) of sausage

AS I MENTIONED EARLIER, PART OF MY FORMATION AS A COOK INCLUDED MY SUMMER IN A GERMAN KITCHEN. While living in that country, I quickly learned that there is much to celebrate in German food, and chief among these celebrations are the vast array of sausages or wursts. Say what you will about German cuisine, but much of what the world knows about sausages is owed to our Teutonic cousins.

Germany and Austria, from which half of my ancestors come, are best known for their white sausages and liver sausages. Liverwurst may be the best known product, although the Midwest of the United States might collapse without the mighty bratwurst. The chauvinism of my Italian friends prevented them from admitting it, but some of the finest street food in the world can be picked up from vendors of wurstchen.

Most of the sausage producers of the world make varieties of head-cheese. While I am unable to get my daughters to try it, I am very fond of this most economic of dishes. When I worked in the kitchen in Hamburg, we were fed twice each shift (a work schedule spanning 3 P.M. to midnight). The second of these meals was called abendbrot (evening bread) and consisted of a mild butterkäse, or butter cheese; volkornbrot, a dense, sour bread full of nutty kernels of grain; and a rich slice of headcheese.

This rich mosaic of bits of meat in its own jelly was a secret vice. It's simple to make. Irma Rombauer (whose *Joy of Cooking* is the one indispensable cookbook I know of) says (as if we all have cooperative butchers), "Have the butcher skin and quarter a calf head. Clean the teeth with a stiff brush and remove ears, brains, eyes, snout and most of the fat..." I won't go any further, except to explain that one cooks the head with some vegetables until the meat falls off the bones. You then gather the meat, strain the stock, concentrate it further, season it, pour it over the meat bits in a mold, and chill until set. Slice and serve. Trust me or try it, it is delicious.

Here, I present some more conventional sausages, including a recipe that may revive the soiled concept of Vienna sausage (although they solved my hunger as a young Boy Scout unable to actually live off the land without a can or two). You'll find that these are far better than the pale versions found in your grocery store.

A German slachtplatte, or butcher's plate, is a perfect way to serve a variety of sausages.

BOCKWURST

Like many of the great German white sausages, bockwurst is composed of veal with some milk. This one is best when very finely ground, and I recommend emulsifying the forcemeat with a food processor. If you do not have a food processor, you can put all of the ingredients through the fine disk of your grinder two or three times.

INGREDIENTS

1¾ pounds (784 g) veal

¼ pound (112 g) unsalted pork fat

¼ cup (45 g) onion, minced

¾ teaspoon ground cloves

½ teaspoon white pepper

2 teaspoons fresh parsley, minced

½ teaspoon sea salt

1 egg, beaten

1 cup (240 mL) milk

4 feet (1.2 m) of prepared hog casing

METHOD

Par freeze the meat and fat. Have the grinder and stuffing attachments sterile and assembled. Load the casing onto the stuffing horn and set aside. Have all ingredients ready and arrayed adjacent to your work surface.

Slice the meat and fat into 1-inch (2.5 cm) slabs. Stack the slabs, then cut again into finger-size pieces. Grind the meat and fat together using the fine disk for your grinder or grinder attachment.

In a large mixing bowl that has been thoroughly cleaned in soapy water and scalded with boiling water, mix the ground meat and fat with all remaining ingredients. Using your hands, reach across the ingredients, grasp a handful, and push it down through the center of the mass. Turn bowl a quarter turn and repeat. Continue until well mixed.

Place the mixed forcemeat into your food processor with a steel blade. Process the forcemeat until it is emulsified and resembles a fine-grained paste. If you do not have a food processor, regrind the forcemeat two or three times through the fine disk of your grinder.

Stuff the completed forcemeat firmly into the casings. Twist the sausage into 4-inch (10 cm) links. Since you will be making links, remember to leave some slack in the casing by understuffing slightly to prevent the casing from bursting when you twist the sausage. Remove any air pockets by piercing with a clean needle.

To cook, boil for 30 minutes. If you are not eating these immediately after cooking, wrap and store the sausages in the refrigerator for up to five days, then reheat when ready to serve.

YIELD: Approximately 2 pounds (896 g) of sausage

BRATWURST

For a summer meal, grilled brats accompanied by potato salad, sauerkraut, mustard, and beer are unbeatable. Come to think of it, this meal may be necessary to the full enjoyment of football tailgate parties as well.

INGREDIENTS

- 1½ pounds (672 g) pork butt
- ⅔ pound (297 g) veal
- ¼ cup (58 g) white bread, no crust
- ¾ cups (180 mL) milk
- 1 teaspoon salt
- ¼ teaspoon white pepper
- ¼ teaspoon mace
- ¼ teaspoon crumbled marjoram
- 4 feet (1.2 m) of prepared hog casing

METHOD

Par freeze the meats. Soak the bread in the milk until the bread is soft. Drain the bread, reserving the milk, and set aside.

Have the grinder and stuffing attachments sterile and assembled. Load the casing onto the stuffing horn and set aside. Have all ingredients ready and arrayed adjacent to your work surface.

Slice the meats into 1-inch (2.5 cm) slabs. Stack the slabs, then cut again into finger-size pieces. Grind the meats together using the coarse disk for your grinder or grinder attachment. You can emulsify the meat in a food processor with a steel blade if you wish, processing until the meats resemble a fine-grained paste. However, I prefer to grind the meats coarse for a chunky consistency.

Place the meat and all remaining ingredients in a large mixing bowl that has been thoroughly cleaned in soapy water and scalded with boiling water. Using your hands, reach across the ingredients, grasp a handful, and push it down through the center of the mass. Turn bowl a quarter turn and repeat. Continue until well mixed.

Stuff the completed forcemeat firmly into the casings. Twist the sausage into 4-inch (10 cm) links. Since you will be making links, remember to leave some slack in the casing by understuffing slightly to prevent the casing from bursting when you twist the sausage. Remove any air pockets by piercing them with a clean needle.

You may poach the sausage for 20 minutes (see the directions for Poaching on page 38), then fry the brats just before eating. However, I prefer and highly recommend them grilled fresh. You can wrap and store the cooled poached sausage in the refrigerator for up to five days, and in the freezer for three months.

YIELD: Approximately 2½ pounds (1.2 kg) of sausage

LIVERWURST

No discussion of German sausage is complete without this delicatessen standby. As a college student in New York City, I often ate a bagel covered with a thick slice of liverwurst that was slathered in mustard and topped with Bermuda onion for breakfast. As well as satisfying my hunger, it helped get me a seat on the subway.

For this sausage, you really need a casing larger than hog casings. If you are unable to find hog bungs, make a muslin casing as follows: Obtain unbleached muslin and cut a piece 8 by 12 inches (20 x 30 cm). Fold it lengthwise and, leaving an ⅛-inch (.3 cm) border, stitch the open side and one end to form a sleeve. Turn the sleeve inside out so that the stitching is on the inside. If you suspect that the muslin has been sized with glue, soak the casing in plain water and wring it out, letting it dry thoroughly before stuffing.

INGREDIENTS

1 pound (448 g) pork butt

OR,

¾ pound (336 g) lean pork loin and ¼ pound (112 g) unsalted pork fat

1 pound (448 g) fresh pork liver

1 large yellow onion, minced

1½ teaspoons sea salt

¼ cup (35 g) powdered milk

1 teaspoon white pepper

2 teaspoons paprika

1 teaspoon sugar

½ teaspoon crumbled marjoram

½ teaspoon ground coriander

¼ teaspoon mace

¼ teaspoon allspice

¼ teaspoon cardamom

Muslin casing or hog bung

YIELD: Approximately 2 pounds (896 g) of sausage

METHOD

Par freeze the meats and fat. At all times keep the ingredients quite cold, refrigerating when necessary. Have the grinder and stuffing attachments sterile and assembled. Load the casing onto the stuffing horn and set aside. Have all ingredients ready and arrayed adjacent to your work surface.

Slice the meats and fat into 1-inch (2.5 cm) slabs. Stack the slabs, then cut again into finger-size pieces. Grind the meats and fat together using the fine disk for your grinder or grinder attachment.

Place the ground meat, fat, and remaining ingredients in a large mixing bowl that has been thoroughly cleaned in soapy water and scalded with boiling water. Using your hands, reach across the ingredients, grasp a handful, and push it down through the center of the mass. Turn bowl a quarter turn and repeat. Continue until well mixed.

Place the mixed forcemeat into a food processor with a steel blade. Process the forcemeat until it is emulsified and resembles fine-grained paste. If you do not have a food processor, regrind the forcemeat through the fine disk of your grinder two or three times. Refrigerate the emulsified mixture for 30 minutes. Since the mixture is sticky, it is easier to pack it into the muslin casing if it is chilled.

To stuff, fold back the open end of the muslin casing and pack the forcemeat into it as firmly as you can, leaving approximately a ½-inch (1.3 cm) seam allowance at the top of the bag. Either sew the top end shut or, using pliers and strong wire, wrap the wire around the end. Whether you sew the end or wrap with wire, make sure the end is tied off very tightly to prevent any forcemeat from seeping out as the sausage cooks.

In a large pot, boil enough water to cover the sausage by 2 or 3 inches (5 or 7.5 cm). Immerse the sausage and weight it down with a plate to keep it submerged. When the water returns to a boil, reduce the heat to barely a simmer and cook for 3 hours. When finished, drain the water and cover the sausage with ice water until cool. Refrigerate overnight and remove casing. Wrap and store the liverwurst in the refrigerator, where it will keep for up to 10 days.

VIENNA SAUSAGE

You may poach and refrigerate these sausages once they are made as I suggest below. Or you can preserve them as a confit which is one way to extend the shelf life of the sausage while adding extra flavor. To make a confit, poach the links for 45 minutes, then cool them thoroughly. Place them in a canning jar and cover them with hot melted fat, cover the jar and store in the refrigerator, where the sausages will keep for eight weeks. To serve, reheat them and drain off the fat.

INGREDIENTS

1½ pound (672 g) pork butt

OR,

1 pound (448 g) lean pork loin and ½ pound (224 g) unsalted pork fat

1 pound (448 g) lean beef

½ pound (224 g) veal

2 tablespoons onion, minced

1½ teaspoons sea salt

½ teaspoon cayenne

1 teaspoon paprika

1 teaspoon sugar

1½ teaspoons ground coriander

½ teaspoon mace

½ cup (70 g) powdered milk

½ cup (120 mL) cold water

4 feet (1.2 m) of prepared hog casing

YIELD: Approximately 3 pounds (1.36 kg) of sausage

METHOD

Par freeze the meats and fat. Have the grinder and stuffing attachments sterile and assembled. Load the casing onto the stuffing horn and set aside. Have all ingredients ready and arrayed adjacent to your work surface.

Slice the meats and fat into 1-inch (2.5 cm) slabs. Stack the slabs, then cut again into finger-size pieces. Grind the meats and fat together using the fine disk for your grinder or grinder attachment.

Place the ground meat, fat, and remaining ingredients in a large mixing bowl that has been thoroughly cleaned in soapy water and scalded with boiling water. Using your hands, reach across the ingredients, grasp a handful, and push it down through the center of the mass. Turn bowl a quarter turn and repeat. Continue until well mixed.

Place the mixed forcemeat into a food processor with a steel blade. Process the forcemeat until it is emulsified and resembles fine-grained paste. If you do not have a food processor, regrind the forcemeat through the fine disk of your grinder two or three times. Refrigerate the emulsified mixture for 30 minutes.

Stuff the emulsified forcemeat into the casings. Twist the sausage into 4-inch (10 cm) links. Using kitchen twine, tie off the links between twists. Since you will be making links, remember to leave some slack in the casing by understuffing slightly to prevent the casing from bursting when you twist the sausage. Remove any air pockets by piercing them with a clean needle.

Poach the sausage for 30 minutes (see poaching directions on page 38). After poaching, cool the sausages. Make sure they are dry before wrapping them to store in the refrigerator. They will keep for one week. You may also make a confit as suggested above.

asia, the middle east, and greece

BEFORE I RETURN TO THE UNITED STATES IN THE NEXT SECTION, I WANT TO VISIT THE REST OF THE WORLD. It may be an injustice to the enormous variety of cultures and cuisines outside of Europe to relegate such small space to them. However, this is due in part to my own limited experience, combined with the fact that there are not as many sausages to present. To summarize this chapter, let me quote Spencer Tracy as he regarded the slender Katharine Hepburn, "There's not much there. But what's there is choice."

One limitation in the world of Asian sausage may result from the restricted amount of meat in the overall diet. This can be better understood when you realize that beef was only introduced in the 16th century by European traders. Finally, although there are several indigenous types of sausage throughout Asia, China seems to have gotten it right the first time. I refer to the fact that one sausage, lop cheong, is used throughout Asia, and used far more often than any other variety. It is wonderful and unlike any European sausage.

These Chinese sausages (as they are referred to everywhere) are extremely versatile, and show up sliced along with bowls of rice or noodles, baked or steamed in dough, and in exotic Thai salads. If you've never had them, the recipe for them may alone justify the purchase of this book. I have included the Thai crab and pork si klok as a very good example of a mixed meat and seafood sausage. Be careful—Thai food can burn out your taste buds if you are unaccustomed to highly spiced foods.

The recipe for lamb sausage, merguez, is Tunisian and Algerian, although I first tasted it in a Lebanese restaurant. This style of skinless sausage from North Africa and the Middle East has influenced European cooking. Much of Southern Africa has adopted variations on British and Dutch sausage. Although the bulk of North Africa and the Middle East is Moslem, and therefore they eat no pork, they more than compensate with inventive spicing and lamb.

Greece, which has given us some of the earliest references to sausages, still loves them. The example I have included, keftedakia, is available grilled in the Acropolis in Athens. There are shops in Greece, known as *allantopoleion*, that are devoted to sausages.

This Thai salad, featuring the Asian sausage lop cheong, is a perfect balance of sweet, sour, and spicy flavors. (recipe on page 101)

LOP CHEONG

These sausages are used throughout Asia as we might use ham—in salads, diced in noodle or rice dishes, or sliced into soups. They are unusual in their sweetness, making them quite exotic, savory, and wonderful. I have made them both by grinding the meat and fat and by cubing them. While it is a bit tedious to cube the meat and fat into small uniform bits, the result is much more interesting. When you are finished making these, they will be thoroughly baked and will keep for two weeks in the refrigerator or six months in the freezer. If you buy them at an Asian market, they are cured and dried, and will keep in the refrigerator for two months.

INGREDIENTS

  2 pounds (896 g) lean pork

  ¾ pound (336 g) unsalted pork fat

  3 tablespoons sugar

  2 tablespoons soy sauce

  2 tablespoons sweet rice wine

  2 tablespoons sake

  2 teaspoons salt

  ¼ teaspoon 5-spice powder

  4 feet (1.2 m) of prepared hog casing

YIELD: Approximately 2¾ pounds (1.2 kg) of sausage

METHOD

Par freeze the meat and fat. Preheat your oven to 200°F (95°C). Work quickly and keep ingredients chilled. Have grinder and stuffing attachments sterile and assembled. Load casing onto stuffing horn and set aside. Have all ingredients ready and arrayed adjacent to your work surface.

Beginning with the meat, slice it into ¼-inch (.6 cm) slabs. Stack the slabs, then cut again into ¼-inch (.6 cm) sticks pieces. Align the sticks and cut into cubes. You want to aim for a ¼-inch (.6 cm) dice. Repeat this process with the fat. (See page 28 for the how-to photos illustrating this process.)

In a large mixing bowl that has been thoroughly cleaned in soapy water and scalded with boiling water, combine the diced meat and fat with all remaining ingredients. Use your hands to mix until well mixed.

Stuff the completed forcemeat firmly into the casings. Because the forcemeat is diced rather than ground or emulsified, you want to stuff the sausage firmly, but will need to allow a little slack for making the links to accommodate the chunkier texture. Twist into three-inch (7.5 cm) links. Pierce any air pockets with a clean needle.

Place a baking rack on top of a sheet pan. Arrange the sausages on the rack so they do not touch each other. Place the sausages in the oven and bake at 200°F (95°C) for 5 hours. After 5 hours, turn off the oven and, without opening the oven door, leave the sausages in the oven for another 2 hours. When you remove the sausages from the oven, wipe off any excess fat.

The sausages are ready to eat, or can be kept in the refrigerator or freezer as noted above. These sausages are particularly nice when sliced for stir-fry or steamed.

SI KLOK

These are from Thailand and are meant to be very spicy—you may need to adjust the level of heat to suit your taste. You can make them using all pork or, as presented here, with half pork meat and half pure crabmeat. Although the sausages are normally eaten poached in Thailand, they are delicious sliced and stir-fried or grilled.

INGREDIENTS

- ½ pound (224 g) pork butt, finely ground
- ½ pound (224 g) crabmeat, cooked and shredded
- 2 teaspoons fish sauce
- 2 tablespoons unsweetened coconut milk
- ¼ teaspoon salt
- ¼ teaspoon chili paste
- ⅛ teaspoon black pepper
- 2 tablespoons fresh coriander, minced (never substitute with dried coriander)
- 3 tablespoons regular chunky peanut butter, avoid extra chunky
- 1 clove fresh garlic, minced
- 2 feet (.6 m) of prepared hog casing

METHOD

Par freeze the meat and fat. Have the grinder and stuffing attachments sterile and assembled. Load the casing onto the stuffing horn and set aside. Have all ingredients ready and arrayed adjacent to your work surface.

Slice the meat and fat into 1-inch (2.5 cm) slabs. Stack the slabs, then cut again into finger-size pieces. Grind the meat using the fine disk for your grinder or grinder attachment.

In a large mixing bowl that has been thoroughly cleaned in soapy water and scalded with boiling water, mix the liquids and spices together first. Then add the ground meat, crabmeat, peanut butter, and garlic. Using your hands, reach across the ingredients, grasp a handful, and push it down through the center of the mass. Turn bowl a quarter turn and repeat. Continue until well mixed.

Stuff the completed forcemeat firmly into the casing to form a single link. Tie off the end by making an overhand knot in the casing or by using a short length of kitchen twine. Remove any air pockets by pricking them with a clean needle.

Poach for 30 minutes (see the directions for poaching on page 38). Eat immediately, or cool before wrapping and storing in the refrigerator, where they will keep for one to one and one-half weeks, or in the freezer for three months.

YIELD: Approximately 1 pound (448 g) of sausage

MERGUEZ

One of my favorite restaurants in Washington, D.C.'s polyglot community was a wonderful Lebanese place south of Dupont Circle. Out of the tourists' path, down a flight of stairs in a warm room, it was always full of groups arguing over the politics of the world, while sharing mezze or appetizers Middle Eastern-style.

One of the most delicious dishes was a lamb sausage that was split open and broiled. It was spicy with harissa, a chili condiment popular throughout the Arabic world (and in my house). With a squeeze of lemon juice and a basket of toasted pita bread wedges I was in my element—solving the world's problems over heated discussions and great food.

The sausages may be made with goat or beef, but I far prefer lamb. You can prepare this as a bulk sausage rather than stuffing the forcemeat in a casing.

INGREDIENTS

- 1 pound (448 g) lamb, coarsely ground
- ¾ teaspoon harissa
- OR, if you can't find harissa, a reasonable substitute can be made by mixing ¼ teaspoon ground cumin, ½ teaspoon minced garlic, and ¼ teaspoon cayenne (or more if you dare!)
- ¼ teaspoon black pepper
- ¼ teaspoon salt
- 2 feet (.6 m) of prepared hog casing

METHOD

If grinding your own, par freeze the meat. If stuffing, have the grinder and stuffing attachments sterile and assembled. Load the casing onto the stuffing horn and set aside. Have all ingredients ready and arrayed adjacent to your work surface.

Slice the meat into 1-inch (2.5 cm) slabs. Stack the slabs, then cut again into finger-size pieces. Grind the meat using the coarse disk for your grinder or grinder attachment.

In a large mixing bowl that has been thoroughly cleaned in soapy water and scalded with boiling water, use your hands to mix all the ingredients together.

If stuffing, stuff the completed forcemeat firmly into the casing. Twist the sausage into 3-inch (7.5 cm) links. Since you will be making links, remember to leave some slack in the casing by understuffing slightly to prevent the casing from bursting when you twist the sausage. Remove any air pockets by piercing them with a clean needle.

Poach the sausages lightly for approximately 10 minutes (see the directions for Poaching on page 38), then split and grill. If you are making bulk sausage, form the forcemeat into small patties, and broil or grill until brown and crisp all over.

YIELD: Approximately 1 pound (448 g) of sausage

KEFTEDAKIA

This delicious lamb sausage comes from Greece and may have been the source of inspiration for Epicharmus in 500 B.C., prompting him to write the play I mentioned in the introduction. Try these bulk sausages in souvlaki sandwiches—they are a welcome succulent change from the dried out, overcooked lamb that is most often the standard fare.

INGREDIENTS

- 1 pound (448 g) lamb, coarsely ground (you may also use ground beef)
- 1 small yellow onion, minced
- ¾ teaspoon sea salt
- ¼ teaspoon black pepper
- ¼ teaspoon cinnamon
- ¼ teaspoon allspice
- ½ teaspoon whole anise seed
- 2 teaspoons fresh parsley, minced
- 2 teaspoons fresh mint, chopped (or 1 teaspoon if using dried mint)
- 1 tablespoon freshly grated kefalotiri, or Parmesan cheese
- 1 tablespoon red wine (or better yet, ouzo!)
- 1 large egg, beaten
- Flour for dusting your hands
- Vegetable oil

METHOD

If grinding your own, par freeze the meat. Have the grinder attachments sterile and assembled. Have all ingredients ready and arrayed adjacent to your work surface.

Slice the meat into 1-inch (2.5 cm) slabs. Stack the slabs, then cut again into finger-size pieces. Grind the meat using the coarse disk for your grinder or grinder attachment.

In a large mixing bowl that has been thoroughly cleaned in soapy water and scalded with boiling water, use your hands to mix all but the final two ingredients.

Dust your hands lightly with flour before forming the forcemeat into eight sausage shapes, each approximately 5 inches (12.5 cm) long. Fry the sausages in hot oil until browned all over, then drain on paper towels.

YIELD: Approximately 1 pound (448 g) of sausage

plastic or wood?

The debate continues as to which material is better for use as cutting boards. Non-porous plastic or acrylic boards have an advantage when it comes to cleaning. They can be washed in the dishwasher that will clean them with water that is set at a much higher temperature than water from the tap. Wood, when properly cleaned with hot soapy water, will provide a safe cutting surface. If you prefer using wood boards, you should consider keeping two separate boards; one used only for raw meats and poultry, the other for breads and produce. Whether you use plastic or wood boards, you should discard them once they develop deep nicks or grooves that are hard to clean.

AS A NATIONAL CULTURE, THE UNITED STATES IS OFTEN ACCUSED OF TRYING TO DOMINATE AND REPLACE CULTURES AROUND THE GLOBE. The fact of the matter, apparent in our founding, is that a large part of our existence is an excuse to blend. We are a cultural fusion—and that is supremely apparent in our foods.

Our country grew up with pockets of homesick cooks who would try new and often strange ingredients, in hopes of reproducing the flavors and smells of their own cultures. The result? The hot dog. Our pizza. Biscuits. Sweet potato pie.

Now we are struggling to identify ourselves as having developed a distinctive cuisine, unique to the U.S. And we have produced a recognizable (if not always wonderful) style of cooking and dining. We each have an idea of what we mean when we talk of California cuisine or southern cooking, or a clam bake or New England boiled dinner.

It is true that much of what distinguishes our regional dishes is owed to the attempt to recapture old world flavors with new world exigencies, but what does it matter? If our foods please us and if they help us to celebrate our identity, then they are right. One of the great ways to be who we are happens when we eat what we are. For example, we are never more American than at Thanksgiving or at a ball game.

I'm no statistician but I read with enough avidity to be intrigued by questions like: "How many hot dogs, placed end to end, would it take to circle the globe or take us to the moon and back?" And, do we Americans eat that many in a year?

Well, if the average hot dog is 8 inches (20 cm) long and the earth is 25,000 miles (40,000 km) in circumference, we need to eat far less than one per citizen, or 198 million wieners, to circle the globe. To get to the moon and back, we will need to consume between 14 and 15 hot dogs each—considerably more than needed to surround our planet, but judging by my own personal consumption this past year, it's a reasonable quantity.

Of course, there is a place in our collective sausage cuisine beyond the hot dog. It's estimated that Americans eat over five billion pounds of sausage annually. That is not a misprint. Billion.

Fresh sausage patties are a highlight of this Southern country breakfast. (recipe on page 93)

HOT DOGS

Americans have been eating hot dogs since before the Civil War, though they didn't get their famous nickname until the early 20th century. They are claimed to be descendants from Czechoslovakian parkys, Austrian wieners or German frankfurters (depending on who you talk to). They are offered to us in a selection so broad they almost merit their own section in the supermarket. Originally made from pork, they can now be found made from beef, turkey, and textured vegetable protein (you may have my portion of the latter).

Unless you are very lucky, you eat hot dogs that are skinned before they are packed, giving them little succulence and no snap when you bite into them. If you are lucky (typically in big cities) you can get the old fashioned sort that are a very lowbrow delicacy. I find the good ones to be the greatest street food anywhere.

The ones you can make here will have snap, juice, and texture, while seducing you with the flavor of mace backed with complex spicing. They will not be pink, since I omit food coloring and preservatives—you won't miss them. However, if you *must* have a pink hot dog, try adding a little beet powder for a natural colorant that won't alter the taste. I am including both pork and beef versions, although you may substitute chicken or turkey or a mixture of both.

PORK HOT DOGS

INGREDIENTS

2¼ pounds (1 kg) pork butt

OR,

2 pounds (896 g) lean pork loin and ¼ pound (112 g) unsalted pork fat

½ cup (120 mL) milk

2 teaspoons light corn syrup

½ teaspoon liquid smoke (omit if you are smoking these)

½ cup (90 g) onion, minced

1 tablespoon sea salt

1 tablespoon dry mustard

2 teaspoons ground coriander

1 teaspoon mace

½ teaspoon white pepper

¼ teaspoon celery seeds, ground

4 feet (1.2 kg) of prepared hog casing

YIELD: Approximately 2½ pounds (1.12 kg) of sausage

BEEF HOT DOGS

INGREDIENTS

These satisfy Kosher requirements

1½ pounds (672 g) beef

½ pound (224 g) veal

½ pound (224 g) beef suet

½ cup (120 mL) cold water

1 teaspoon light corn syrup

½ teaspoon liquid smoke (omit if you are smoking these)

½ cup (90 g) onion, minced

2 cloves fresh garlic, minced

1 tablespoon sea salt

1 teaspoon dry mustard

1 teaspoon prepared coarse mustard

2 teaspoons ground coriander

1 teaspoon mace

1 teaspoon paprika

½ teaspoon black pepper

4 feet (1.2 m) of prepared lamb casing

YIELD: Approximately 3 pounds (1.36 kg) of sausage

METHOD

Par freeze the meats and fat. At all times keep the ingredients quite cold, refrigerating when necessary. Have the grinder and stuffing attachments sterile and assembled. Load the casing onto the stuffing horn and set aside. Have all ingredients ready and arrayed adjacent to your work surface.

Slice the meats and fat into 1-inch (2.5 cm) slabs. Stack the slabs, then cut again into finger-size pieces. Grind the meats and fat together using the fine disk for your grinder or grinder attachment.

Mix the liquids with the remaining ingredients before mixing them with the meat and fat. Place the ground meat and fat and remaining ingredients in a large mixing bowl that has been thoroughly cleaned in soapy water and scalded with boiling water. Using your hands, reach across the ingredients, grasp a handful, and push it down through the center of the mass. Turn bowl a quarter turn and repeat. Continue until well mixed.

Place the mixed forcemeat into a food processor with a steel blade. Process the forcemeat until it is emulsified and resembles fine-grained paste. If you do not have a food processor, regrind the forcemeat through the fine disk of your grinder two or three times. Refrigerate the emulsified mixture for 30 minutes.

Stuff the completed forcemeat firmly into the casings. Twist the finished sausage into 7-inch (17.5 cm) links. Since you will be making links, remember to leave some slack in the casing by understuffing slightly to prevent the casing from bursting when you twist the sausage. Remove any air pockets by piercing them with a clean needle.

Poach the sausage for 15 minutes (see the directions for Poaching on page 38). Eat immediately as is, or cook as desired. (I will not presume to tell an American how to cook their hot dogs.) To store, cool, dry, wrap, and refrigerate. They will keep one week in the refrigerator and three months in the freezer. If you have a smoker, smoke at 275°F (135°C) until the sausages reach an internal temperature of 170°F (77°C).

hot dog!

Once known as dachshund sausage or little-dog sausage, hot dogs got their name in 1901 at the New York Polo Grounds. A vendor placed the sausages in buns and called out, "They're red hot," to entice potential customers. A cartoonist heard the phrase, and drew a picture of barking dachshund sausages snuggled in buns. He wasn't sure how to spell dachshund, and penned the caption "Hot Dog!"

happy birthday

Frankfurt-am-Main, Germany, claims to be the birthplace of the hot dog. In 1987 they celebrated its 500th anniversary.

billions!!!

Americans consume approximately 20 billion hot dogs per year. One hundred and fifty million of these are eaten in major league ballparks

CAJUN BOUDIN

I love this sausage which is in a category all its own. My first introduction to this boudin (which in no way resembles the French boudins) was in print. I finally bit into one at a small, informal Cajun restaurant in Bethesda, Maryland, which remains one of my favorite eateries anywhere. No, I'm not giving out the name—it's already too hard to get a seat. Find your own paradise.

Although these need nothing other than beer as an accompaniment, I love a remoulade sauce (see page 121 or a spicy creole mustard. As always, please yourself. (But don't stint on the cayenne!)

INGREDIENTS

- 1 pound (448 g) lean pork and ½ pound (224 g) unsalted pork fat
- ¾ cup (150 g) uncooked rice
- 1 tablespoon sea salt
- ¼ cup (28 g) fresh parsley, minced
- ¾ cup (112 g) scallions, chopped
- 1 teaspoon cayenne
- ½ teaspoon ground black pepper
- ¼ teaspoon allspice
- 3 feet (.9 m) of prepared hog casing

METHOD

Par freeze the meat and fat. Have the grinder and stuffing attachments sterile and assembled. Load the casing onto the stuffing horn and set aside. Have all ingredients ready and arrayed adjacent to your work surface. Cook the rice and allow to cool slightly.

Slice the meat and fat into 1-inch (2.5 cm) slabs. Stack the slabs, then cut again into finger-size pieces. Grind the meat and fat together using the coarse disk for your grinder or grinder attachment.

In a large mixing bowl that has been thoroughly cleaned in soapy water and scalded with boiling water, use your hands to mix the meat and fat with all remaining ingredients.

Stuff the completed forcemeat firmly into the casings. Twist the sausage into 7-inch (18 cm) links. Since you will be making links, remember to leave some slack in the casing by understuffing slightly to prevent the casing from bursting when you twist the sausage. Remove any air pockets by piercing them with a clean needle.

Poach the sausage for 25 minutes (see the directions for Poaching on page 38). Eat immediately, preparing the sausages as you like. To store, rinse, cool, wrap, and refrigerate. The sausages will keep for three to five days. Do not freeze these sausages; the rice will become unpleasantly soft and ruin the texture.

YIELD: Approximately 2 pounds (896 kg) of sausage

SOUTHERN COUNTRY SAUSAGE

I once operated a very sophisticated French bakery in Knoxville, Tennessee, in the old city. The buildings dated back to the mid-19th century, and were layered with history and atmosphere. The crusty, golden baguettes were a hit—except on Saturday morning. As if possessed by the ghosts of their ancestors, anyone not cooking their own breakfast headed out for sausages, biscuits, and gravy. Here is why. This is a spicier version of the bulk breakfast sausage found at the beginning of the book.

INGREDIENTS

2¾ pounds (1.2 kg) pork butt, boned and trimmed of sinew

OR,

2 pounds (896 g) lean pork loin and ¾ pound (336 g) unsalted pork fat

2 teaspoons sea salt

½ teaspoon black pepper

1 tablespoon fresh sage, minced (½ tablespoon if using dried) ½ teaspoon fresh thyme (¼ teaspoon if using dried)

½ teaspoon fresh rosemary (¼ teaspoon if using dried)

½ teaspoon nutmeg

½ teaspoon cloves

½ teaspoon cayenne

1 tablespoon brown sugar

4 feet (1.2 m) of prepared hog casing, if stuffing

METHOD

Par freeze the meat and fat. Have the grinder and stuffing attachments sterile and assembled. If stuffing the sausage, load the casing onto the stuffing horn and set aside. Have all ingredients ready and arrayed adjacent to your work surface.

Slice the meat and fat into 1-inch (2.5 cm) slabs. Stack the slabs, then cut again into finger-size pieces. Grind the meat and fat together using the coarse disk for your grinder or grinder attachment.

In a large mixing bowl that has been thoroughly cleaned in soapy water and scalded with boiling water, mix the meat and fat with all remaining ingredients. Using your hands, reach across the ingredients, grasp a handful, and push it down through the center of the mass. Turn bowl a quarter turn and repeat. Continue until well mixed.

If using as a bulk sausage, cook immediately by forming the forcemeat into patties and frying in a skillet until brown and crisp. (You'll find a milk gravy recipe on page 14 and a recipe for redeye gravy below.) You can also store the forcemeat, wrapping it and keeping in the refrigerator for three days. Or wrap and store in the freezer for three months.

If you are stuffing the forcemeat, stuff firmly into the casings. Twist the sausage into 4-inch (10 cm) links. Since you will be making links, remember to leave some slack in the casing by understuffing slightly to prevent the casing from bursting when you twist the sausage. Remove any air pockets by piercing them with a clean needle. To store, follow the directions above for storing the bulk sausage.

YIELD: Approximately 2¾ pounds (1.2 kg) of sausage

REDEYE GRAVY

You'll find that this variant of the traditional milk-and-flour sausage gravy is kinder to your waistline. When you have fried up a "mess" of breakfast or southern country sausage, pour off all but a small bit of fat and immediately deglaze the pan with two or three tablespoons of strong black coffee. Salt to taste.

sausage cuisine

THERE ARE MANY GLORIOUS MEALS BASED ON SAUSAGE—and the cultures of the world show little limitation in what they have done to serve this staple. You would have to be marooned on a desert island to not have experienced many of these recipes.

Some cultural signatures are simply arrays of a variety of sausage and other meats served seasonally. These include, from Alsace Lorraine, choucroute garnie served with sauerkraut and flavored with juniper berries, and the hearty German slachtplatte, or butcher's plate (*schlacten*—to butcher). These dishes are a source of great pride.

Other sausage dishes are rich and complex stews, such as cassoulet from France; gumbo, a Cajun interpretation of an African okra stew; bigos which is a Polish game stew with sausages and mushrooms—and many others. Sausage often is best served simply—grilled or poached—and shines with great side dishes and relishes. At a Christmas dinner once, a patriotic Swede confessed that the julkorv (Christmas potato sausage) was "only so-so until served with a great mustard." Sometimes the meeting of condiment and sausage are unexpected (try a dab of bitter orange marmalade with a juicy garlic sausage) and ultimately delightful.

I have included several main dishes and accompaniments in this recipe section. But keep in mind the purpose of books like this is to launch you into your own creative uses of seasonal provender. Once you've learned the fundamentals of sausage making and the methods of cooking them, apply the techniques on your shopping trips to search for ingredients that will help you invent new combinations.

In many ways sausage is a blank canvas, and we are like young art students. We begin by copying and trying to reproduce the classics and, if we wish (and I wish you to do so), we then begin to find our own style, subtle and tender or bold and exciting. Enjoy your favorites, but stretch occasionally. Remember to follow the underlying theme of this book, to please yourself (and your fortunate guest!). Here are some dishes that I love.

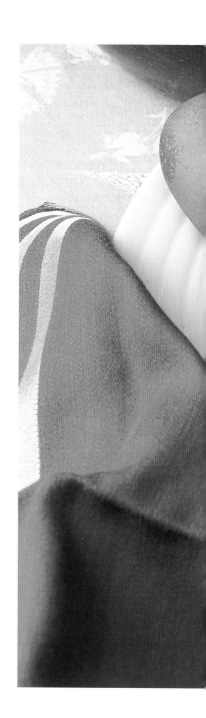

delicious
sausage dishes

Caldo verde
(recipe on page 96)

CALDO VERDE
KALE AND POTATO SOUP

Hearty, healthy, and quick to prepare, this soup is a way to enjoy your vegetables with a spicy kick— even if you're running late. Served with crusty bread, it becomes a satisfying one-dish meal.

INGREDIENTS

   1 pound (448 g) kale

   1 pound (448 g) potatoes

1½ quarts (1.4 L) water

   2 tablespoons olive oil

½ pound (224 g) garlic sausage
   or chorizo, sliced, browned,
   and drained of fat

   Salt and pepper to taste

METHOD

Tear the kale leaves into bite-sized pieces and mince the stalks. Peel the potatoes if you like (I do not), and slice them into chunks. Place the minced kale stalks in salted water and bring to a boil.

Add the potatoes and lower to a simmer for 20 minutes or until tender. Using a slotted spoon, remove the potatoes, mash them, then return them to the pot. Add the kale leaves and sausage, and cook until the kale is tender. This takes approximately 5 to 10 minutes, although it may take a little longer.

YIELD: Four servings

STUFFED ONIONS

We don't often think about onions taking a starring role in a dish—most often they are a featured player. I prefer the stronger taste of yellow onion to complement the spicy chorizo. Some of you may prefer using one of the varieties of milder, sweet onions that are readily available in the early summer.

INGREDIENTS

12 large onions
Cooking oil

1 pound (448 g) chorizo, skinned

½ cup (90 g) carrot, minced

½ cup (90 g) celery, minced

1 cup (70 g) bread crumbs

METHOD

Preheat the oven to 450°F (230°C). Carefully peel the onions, leaving them whole. In a large pot of boiling water, parboil the onions for 10 minutes, drain, and cool. Cut a slice off the root end and scoop out approximately three-quarters of each onion.

Place the onions, hollowed side up, in a baking dish while you prepare the filling.

In a skillet, heat a small amount of cooking oil and fry the chorizo, breaking it apart with a wooden spoon as it cooks. When the sausage is an even color through-out, cooked but not brown, add the vegetables and cook on low heat until the vegetables are soft, approx-imately 10 minutes.

Using a slotted spoon to allow as much fat as possible to drain out, scoop out portions of the sausage and vegetable mixture, and fill each hollowed-out onion just to the rim. Top each onion with bread crumbs.

Pour enough water in a baking pan to come up to just ½ inch (1.5 cm) around the filled onions and bake for 20 minutes.

YIELD: 12 servings

JAMBALAYA

The origins of this dish are draped in Spanish moss. Chef Paul Prudhomme credits the French and Yoruba languages for giving this dish its name—*jambon* (ham) *a la ya* (Yoruba for rice)—hence *Jamb-a-la-ya*. For the rest of us, it is simply a highly spiced rice dish with ham and almost any meat and, often, tomatoes. I say eat it all up.

INGREDIENTS

¼ cup (60 mL) cooking oil

¼ pound (112 g) ham, diced

1 pound (448 g) sausage, sliced

1½ cups (270 g) onions, chopped

1½ cups (270 g) celery, chopped

1 cup (180 g) green pepper, chopped

4 cloves fresh garlic, minced

2 bay leaves

1 teaspoon cayenne

1 teaspoon white pepper

1 teaspoon black pepper

1 teaspoon thyme

1 teaspoon cumin, ground

1 teaspoon salt

2 cups (448 g) uncooked rice

1 quart (.95 L) stock, beef or chicken

1 pound (448 g) large shrimp, peeled and deveined

METHOD

Heat the oil in a large skillet or heavy pot, and cook the ham and sausage until they begin to crisp at the edges. Add all the vegetables and seasonings, and cook, stirring frequently, for 10 minutes.

Stir in the rice and add the stock. Bring to a boil, reduce heat to low, cover, and cook for 20 minutes, until rice is done. Jambalaya is often served while the rice is still a little underdone and slightly crunchy. Please yourself—but please, add the shrimp at the last minute, adding a little water or stock if the rice is too dry, and cook just until the shrimp colors all the way through.

YIELD: 8 servings

sausage feast

A RECIPE FOR CELEBRATION

WHILE THIS IS NOT A STANDARD COOKING RECIPE—one that provides the means for making a prepared dish—it is a recipe nonetheless. Consider the following as a guideline for assembling the ingredients of your life and shaping them into a feast for the soul.

One irresistible impulse that often overtakes the home chef (a cook with pretensions) is to fill the table to groaning under the weight of one's culinary wizardry. With a little help, sausage can be the star to which you can hitch your wagon. First, let's find an excuse.

Think of the four days each year during which the perfection of the season causes us (wherever we live) to exclaim (whether we are extroverts or alone), "This is why we live here!" At these moments, in our respective perfect worlds, we need a feast. A winter/summer solstice bacchanal, Bastille Day, Guy Faulk's day, the Fourth, the Ides of whatever, the Nones of October, the Day of the Dead, the author's birthday.

What is it that characterizes a feast? They are most often gatherings designed to remember and honor people and events that have great meaning for a community. One encyclopedia suggests that feasts often are celebrations of cherished folkways. They are part of what expresses the whole concept of community. Feasts have always (though no longer exclusively) been associated with harvests or plantings to celebrate the bounty or bless the undertaking.

Surely, you can think of something worth celebrating. When you've seen the first fireflies in summer, or you can calculate the day when the leaves will be their most colorful, Bloomsday, D-day, April 15th, Juneteenth, the day you stopped smoking... come on over. I'll do the food.

Nowhere is the admonishment to please yourself more useful than in the structure of your own personal feast day. I will give you some ideas. Think in terms of critical mass. How many guests are necessary to ignite a festive day? I personally believe children are required (at least two in strollers, up to five in the running around, ungoverned stage, and a pinch of teens to be publicly aloof while privately pleased to be here). It helps if at least two supervising parents are present, one to tell the stories and the other to edit and correct. The grown children will have to drive a long way or, better still, fly in to get there. And don't forget institutional memory, you need an elder or two, the crustier the better.

Now, where were we? Food. Sausage. At least three varieties cooked in three different methods. Three salads or cold dishes. One soup (three in Winter). Three breads (crusty French, homemade biscuits, and either cornbread or pita). Three hot vegetable dishes and one or two starches. Something with pasta and something with potatoes. Rice is good, too. Dips and spreads and sauces in abundance.

If it is at all possible, have everyone bring something. Some dish will not turn out well, but there will be plenty for everyone. Resist, if you can, the temptation to sculpt something out of sausage meat. Never permit guests to make costumes that include sausage as an element. Be certain to have storage containers and sturdy freezer bags, because guests should never depart a feast without extras.

Finally, arrange as much of the cooking to be done in advance as possible—except the sausage. Casseroles and stews are one thing, but don't grill or poach sausage in advance. While sausage makes fine leftovers, the fresh-off-the-grill juice and snap are the acme only you, the home sausage maker, can provide.

THAI SAUSAGE SALAD

The seductive combinations of sweet, hot, and sour with crisp and yielding textures and exotic herbiness make this salad an adventure.

DRESSING INGREDIENTS

1 cup (240 mL) lime juice

½ cup (100 g) sugar

¾ cup (180 mL) fish sauce

1 jalapeno or serrano chile, minced

4 cloves of fresh garlic, minced

2 bulbs lemongrass, minced

SALAD INGREDIENTS

3 heads Romaine lettuce, torn into small pieces

3 large cucumbers, peeled and sliced

1 red onion, peeled and thinly sliced

6 carrots, shredded

1 cup (180 g) radishes, sliced

1 cup (50 g) fresh coriander leaves

¼ cup (12 g) fresh mint, chopped

¼ cup (12 g) fresh basil, chopped

1 pound (448 g) sliced, browned, and drained lop cheong sausage

METHOD

Mix the dressing ingredients and set aside. Slice the sausage diagonally and place them in a medium-sized frying pan. Add approximately ¼ inch (.6) of water to the pan. Cook the sausages, allowing the water to evaporate. Continue cooking the sausages until they are lightly and evenly browned, then drain. Toss the salad, add sausage and dressing, and serve immediately.

YIELD: 6–8 servings

SHU MAI—POT STICKERS

These are called pot stickers because that is what they do. These filled dumplings are cooked in a small amount of water and oil. First they steam, which cooks the filling and makes the dough wrapper silken and supple. Then, when the water has cooked off, their bases fry in the oil to form a crust on the bottom.

Shu Mai are one form of *dim sum*, which are among the great delights of Chinese cooking. Whole meals can be composed of these packaged fillings which are fried, deep fried, steamed, poached, boiled, or baked. They are the source of such Italian delights as tortellini and ravioli. I offer you a more classic recipe for which I have substituted a mild sausage for the traditional ground or chopped pork. My advice is to assemble a crew around the kitchen table and make a variety of these dumplings.

For the dough wrapper, you may buy wonton skins or egg roll wrappers typically offered in the grocery store where Asian vegetables are displayed. I am including a recipe for the dough because I think the result is better.

DOUGH

INGREDIENTS

   2 cups (280 g) all-purpose flour

   1 cup (240 mL) boiling water

METHOD

In a large bowl, combine the flour and boiling water, mixing as well as you can. Let the mixture rest for 20 minutes, then knead it until it is smooth and soft (use as much flour as you need to work the dough).

Roll it into a sausage, and cut it into 16 equal pieces. Pat each piece into rounds, and roll them into 4-inch (10 cm) circles. Flour each piece and stack them, covering them with a damp towel until you need them.

POT STICKERS

INGREDIENTS

   1 recipe of the dough described above, or enough wonton skins to make 24 dumplings

 ½ pound (224 g) pork, or chicken and pork sausage

   2 cloves fresh garlic (unless the sausage has lots of garlic already), minced

   2 slices fresh ginger, peeled and minced

   1 scallion, finely chopped

   1 cup (180 g) bok choy or any variety Chinese cabbage, finely chopped

   1 tablespoon cornstarch dissolved in ¼ cup (60 mL) of water

   1 tablespoon sesame oil

      Salt and black pepper to taste

   2 tablespoons vegetable oil, plus, 1 cup (240 mL) boiling water mixed with 2 tablespoons of oil

POT STICKERS METHOD

Mix meat with the garlic, ginger, and scallion. Sprinkle approximately ¼ teaspoon salt on the chopped bok choy, and let it sit for 5 minutes. Squeeze out excess moisture and add to the meat mixture. Add cornstarch and sesame oil, and mix thoroughly, adding salt and pepper to taste.

When you have made the hot water dough, cut it into 24 pieces, rolling them into 3-inch (7.5 cm) circles. Shaping pot stickers can be as simple or as complex as you want. The traditional shape is made as follows: Lay a circle of dough in the palm of your hand. On one edge pinch the dough together to form little pleats so that the dough forms a kind of shell-shaped cup. Place a teaspoonful of filling in the cup and seal the unpleated edge to the pleated edge (you may need to moisten the dough so it will adhere). Gently, hold the dumplings seam side up and tamp them on the counter to form a flat bottom so that they stand up easily. Set the finished dumplings on a flour-dusted surface spaced to not touch each other. When all the dumplings are finished, they can be frozen on a cookie sheet and then bagged until needed.

When you are ready to cook them, first prepare a dipping sauce. I like them with the traditional sauce that combines Chinese black vinegar and minced garlic. They are also delicious with a sushi dip of soy sauce and a little prepared wasabi. All of these items are available in oriental groceries and, increasingly, at most supermarkets.

To cook, heat 2 tablespoons oil in a heavy skillet or a wok, and place all of the dumplings upright in the oil. Pour in the oil and boiling water mixture, and reduce the heat to medium. Loosen any dumplings that have stuck to the pan, then cover the pan and cook for 10 minutes to steam them. Remove the cover and boil off the remaining water to fry the bottoms golden brown.

YIELD: 24 dumplings

HUEVOS RANCHEROS

This is the real thing. Making your own salsa ranchera seals the authenticity. If you want to go even further, try making your own corn tortillas! Serve this egg, sausage, and cheese dish anytime—it's too good to save only for weekend brunch.

INGREDIENTS

- 1 large ripe tomato
- 1 chile serrano
- 1 clove fresh garlic, minced
- 1 tablespoon peanut oil
- 1 thick slice of onion, minced
  Salt to taste
- 2 tablespoons peanut oil
- 2 corn tortillas per serving
- 4 inches (10 cm) of chorizo, skinned, per serving
- 2 eggs per serving
- 2 tablespoons crumbled queso fresca or feta cheese per serving

METHOD

First make the salsa ranchera. Line a broiling pan with tin foil. Broil the tomato until slightly blackened. Be careful to avoid placing the broiler too close to the flame (or element) or it will burn the tomato before it is warmed through. In a hot, dry pan, toast the serrano for about one minute. Blend the tomato, serrano, and garlic in a blender until smooth.

In a skillet, heat 1 tablespoon of peanut oil and cook the onion until translucent. Add the blended ingredients and heat through, cooking until just slightly thickened. Salt to your taste and set aside. This is enough for four servings.

Heat the 2 tablespoons of oil until hot. Fry the tortillas briefly so that they heat through and soften but not until they become crisp. In the same oil, fry the chorizo, breaking it apart as it browns. Remove the sausage from the pan with a slotted spoon to drain the fat.

In the same pan, fry the eggs until set. (Cook them to your preference; I like formed whites with crisp edges and a still runny yolk.)

On a single serving gratin (or any plate that you can stick under the broiler flame or element) place the tortillas, cover them with the chorizo, the eggs, and a generous portion of the salsa ranchera. Sprinkle some of the cheese on top and place under broiler just until the cheese begins to melt.

YIELD: 1 serving is 2 eggs and 2 tortillas

GREEN BEAN, TOMATO, AND SAUSAGE SOUP

This lovely soup recipe was passed to me by a dear friend who got it from a much loved (and now defunct) local restaurant. It combines the intense green of the beans, the acid bite of good canned tomatoes, and the smoky background of sausage. My friend prefers kielbasa but I find any smoked or liquid-smoke flavored sausage equally delicious.

INGREDIENTS

- 2 tablespoons butter
- 1 cup (180 g) onion, chopped
- 1 clove fresh garlic, minced
- ½ pound (224 g) smoked sausage, sliced, browned, and drained
- ½ pound (224 g) green beans, sliced diagonally into 1½-inch (4 cm) lengths
- 2 cups (448 g) canned tomatoes, preferably imported Italian
- 1 cup (240 mL) tomato juice from the can
- 1 cup (240 mL) stock, either vegetable or chicken
- 2 cups (480 mL) water
- 1 bay leaf
- 1 teaspoon chili powder
- Worcestershire sauce, a dash
- Salt and pepper to taste

METHOD

Melt the butter over medium heat in a soup pot, and cook the onion and garlic until they are soft but not browned, approximately 10 minutes. Add remaining ingredients, bring to a boil, then reduce to a simmer and cook for ½ hour.

Refrigerate overnight to allow flavors to mingle and develop. Reheat, adjust seasoning, and serve. If the flavor needs brightening, add a tablespoon each of vinegar and good quality olive oil.

YIELD: 4–6 servings

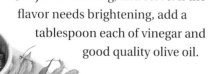

SAUSAGE BALLS AND RED SAUCE

This sauce is perfect to dress up a pasta or to fill in a great meatball submarine sandwich. All you have to do for an unbeatable sub is to top a butterflied torpedo roll with the meatballs and sauce, then lay on slices of provolone cheese. Run the sub under the broiler to melt the cheese—then grab a bib!

INGREDIENTS

- ⅓ cup (80 mL) milk
- 1 thick slice bread
- 1 pound (448 g) fresh bulk sausage meat
- 1 tablespoon fresh parsley, minced
- 1 egg
- 3 tablespoons Parmesan cheese, grated
- Olive oil
- Breadcrumbs, dry and plain (unflavored)
- 2 cups (448 g) canned tomatoes, preferably imported Italian, chopped with juice
- Salt and pepper to taste

METHOD

In a saucepan, put the bread in the milk and bring to a boil. Remove from the heat and mash the bread with a fork, blending it into the milk. Cool.

Combine the meat, parsley, egg, Parmesan cheese, and 1 tablespoon of the olive oil in a mixing bowl. Once the bread and milk mixture is cool, gently combine it with the ingredients in the bowl.

Form the mixture into small 1 to 1½-inch (2.5 to 4 cm) balls. Try not to compact the meatballs as you shape them. Once formed, roll them in the breadcrumbs.

In a large skillet with a cover, heat ¼ inch (.6 cm) of oil until hot. Brown the meatballs on all sides, then reduce the heat to a simmer. Tilt the pan carefully to skim as much of the fat as you can. Add the tomatoes and juice, turning the meatballs to coat them thoroughly. Cover the pan and simmer for 20 minutes or until the sauce has formed and thickened.

YIELD: 4–6 servings

BIGOS

Poland is a country whose hardworking people love their foods. Mushrooms and sausages top the pantheon of cultural cooking. Kielbasa, as I mentioned earlier, simply means sausage, although we take it to mean a loop of thick, garlicky, smoked sausage. Bigos is one of those enormous pots of everything that each culture offers us. In this case it is a hunter's stew. I am not clear whether Bigos was prepared to take along on the hunt, made during the hunt, or created from the success of the hunt. Nevertheless, this dish has as many possibilities as your larder.

INGREDIENTS

- 5   slices of slab bacon, cut into 1-inch (2.5 cm) pieces
- 1½ pounds (672 g) pork, cubed (you can substitute or add lamb, venison, rabbit, and chicken)
- 1   pound (448 g) garlic sausage, smoked or smoke flavored
- ½   medium head of green cabbage, chopped
- 2   onions, chopped
- 2   Granny Smith apples, cored and sliced
- 2   cups (448 g) sauerkraut, rinsed and squeezed of excess moisture
- 1   cup (340 g) tomato paste
- 2   cups (480 mL) beef stock
- 1   ounce (28 g) dried mushrooms, soaked, drained, and chopped (reserve the soaking liquid)
-     4 bay leaves
-     Salt and pepper to taste

METHOD

In a large, heavy pot, fry the bacon to render the fat. Remove the bacon and set aside. In the bacon fat, brown the other meats and sausage. Remove the meats and set aside with the bacon.

To the meat drippings, add the cabbage, reduce the heat, and cook for 10 minutes to soften and blend flavors. Add the onion and cook for another 10 minutes. Finally, add the apple and sauerkraut and cook for an additional 5 minutes.

Add all the remaining ingredients to the pot, including the meats, the mushrooms, and soaking water. Cover the pot and simmer for 1 hour. Uncover the pot, skim the fat and adjust the seasonings to taste. You may refrigerate overnight if you like to facilitate removing the fat and for strengthening the flavors.

YIELD: 8 servings

TIP: *Rinse dried mushrooms well before soaking to remove any residual grit. After soaking, remove the mushrooms and reserve the liquid. When adding the liquid to a recipe, place a paper coffee filter in a strainer and pour the liquid through the filter to catch any grit from the soaking.*

gratin de pommes de terre et saucisson

108   making great sausage

GRATIN DE POMMES DE TERRE ET SAUCISSON

POTATOES AU GRATIN WITH SAUSAGE

On an ordinary night, your family might just refer to these as cheesy potatoes. But dress them up with sausage, a little white wine, a fresh salad, and candlelight, and they become a French delight.

INGREDIENTS

3 cups (448 g) sliced, cooked potatoes

1 cup (90 g) onions, minced

1 pound (448 g) sliced, browned, and drained mild sausage (such as boudins blancs)

3 eggs

1½ cup (360 mL) cream

Salt and pepper to taste

¼ cup (30 g) grated Gruyere (or Swiss cheese)

Butter

METHOD

Preheat oven to 375˚F (190˚C). In an ovenproof dish or pie pan, arrange layers of potatoes, onions, and sausage, ending with a layer of potatoes.

Mix the eggs and cream with the salt and pepper, and pour into the dish. Sprinkle the top with cheese and dot with butter. Bake for 30 minutes or until the cheese begins to brown.

YIELD: 4 servings

PEA SOUP AND JULKORV

I am told that the Swedes prefer their pea soup, which they love, very thick. Whatever the particular preference, the combination of pea soup, julkorv (Christmas potato sausage), and cold weather offers warmth and security—the very essence of comfort food. I prefer the sausage poached and served separately (rather than cooked in the soup) with a good mustard or mustard thinned with a little sour cream (fresh dill wouldn't hurt).

I believe that making soup at any time is a healing experience. If you have no current emotional wounds or soft sadnesses to heal, make a soup anyway, and find someone who needs comforting. If you can arrange to do this in the winter on a long twilit afternoon, you will probably have the beginnings of a short story (to paraphrase the usual) about man's humanity to man. At the worst, you'll have a lovely, comforting meal.

INGREDIENTS

2 cups (400 g) split peas
1 meaty ham bone
½ cup (90 g) onions, minced
½ cup (90 g) carrots, minced
1 cup (180 g) celery, minced
1 bay leaf
Julkorv, enough to serve at least one link to each guest

METHOD

Wash and soak the peas for several hours or over-night. Do not discard the soaking liquid. Place the peas and the soaking liquid in a heavy pot, along with the ham bone and enough extra water to make about 2½ quarts (2.4 L). Cover and simmer for 3 hours.

Add the remaining ingredients and cook for an additional ½ hour. Just before you add the vegetables, bring a pot of water to a simmer and poach the sausage for 20 minutes. Sköl!

YIELD: 8 servings

LENTILS COOKED WITH SAUSAGE

Lentils are peasant food that kings love. I am, depending on the day, either or both. I particularly like to use tiny, French Dupuy lentils which work well with this dish that I call a stewp—that is to say a soup that is thick enough to serve on a plate, but not quite a stew. Use smoked sausage, or sausage flavored with liquid smoke, to add a hearty note.

INGREDIENTS

1 tablespoon olive oil
¼ pound (112 g) sausage, diced small
1 cup (180 g) each, carrots, onions, and celery, chopped
1 pound (448 g) lentils, washed and drained (they do not need a preliminary soak)
1 bay leaf
½ teaspoon thyme
Salt and pepper to taste
2½ quarts (2.4 L) water (or half water, half chicken or beef stock)
½ pound (224 g) sausage (particularly those that are smoked or flavored with liquid smoke), sliced

METHOD

Heat the oil in a heavy pot and brown the diced sausage. Add the vegetables and cook until softened, about 10 minutes. Add the lentils, herbs, and water/stock, and simmer for 3 hours or until lentils are softened but not mushy. When the lentils are done, brown the remaining sausage and add it to the soup before serving.

YIELD: 4 servings

CASSOULET

First invite a dozen friends, select a favorite wine, and purchase a few loaves of crusty bread. This elegant peasant dish is bound to inspire convivial conversation and camaraderie.

INGREDIENTS

- 1½ pounds (672 g) dry white beans, picked over and soaked in water overnight
- 1 yellow onion, peeled
- 4 whole cloves
- 2 sprigs each, fresh parsley, rosemary, and thyme
- 1 bay leaf
- 2 carrots, peeled and thinly sliced
- 1½ quarts (1.4 L) homemade or low-salt chicken stock
- 6 tablespoons duck fat or lard
- 6 cloves of fresh garlic, smashed with a knife blade
- ¾ pound (340 g) salt pork, rinsed several times in clean water and cubed
- 1 pound (448 g) lamb, cubed
- 1 pound (448 g) pork loin, cubed
- 1 pound (448 g) garlic sausage (saussison a l'ail, salsiccie or luganega)
- 1 pound (448 g) duck confit, fat reserved, or, 1 duck cut into serving pieces
- 2 large onions, chopped
- 1 can of tomatoes, 20 ounces (560 g)
- Breadcrumbs (optional)

METHOD

First, drain and rinse the soaked beans and place in a large casserole or ovenproof pot. (All of the ingredients will eventually be in this one pot.) Stick the 4 whole cloves into the peeled onion and add to the pot along with the fresh herbs, bay leaf, carrots, and stock. Bring to a boil, lower heat, and simmer during the next step, which will take approximately 45 minutes.

Preheat the oven to 350°F (175°C). In a large skillet, heat the fat and sauté the garlic until soft, and add to pot. Then, successively brown the salt pork, lamb, pork, sausages, duck, and onions. Drain the fat after browning each of these and before adding to the pot.

Add tomatoes to the pot, push the meats below the beans, and place in oven. Bake for 1½ hours. During this period, stir occasionally, pushing the meats below surface. If you like, for the last 20 minutes, top the mixture with bread crumbs.

YIELD: 12 servings

CHOUCROUTE BRAISÉE A L'ALSACIENNE GARNIE

BRAISED SAUERKRAUT WITH MEATS, ALSATIAN STYLE

Discover the delicious blending of French and German cooking traditions with this Alsatian dish. The slow cooking of the sauerkraut with the other ingredients renders it sweet and savory—a perfect companion to the sausage and meat.

INGREDIENTS

2 pounds (896 g) sauerkraut

½ pound (224 g) thick sliced bacon, cut into 2-inch (5 cm) pieces

¼ cup (60 mL) vegetable oil

½ cup (90 g) sliced carrots

1 cup (180 g) sliced onions

4 sprigs fresh parsley

6 whole peppercorns

10 juniper berries

1 cup (240 mL) dry white wine

1 quart (.95 L) chicken stock

6 pork chops, thick-cut

1 pound (448 g) garlic sausage

6 slices cooked ham, thinly sliced

METHOD

Soak and drain the sauerkraut in three changes of water—soak for 20 minutes, drain, then soak again, repeat. Preheat oven to 325°F (165°C). Blanch the bacon by simmering in water for 10 minutes, then drain.

Heat the oil in a large lidded ovenproof pot, and cook the bacon, carrots, and onions for 10 minutes (do not brown). Stir in the sauerkraut, and cook, covered, for 10 more minutes. Add herbs and liquids to the pot, restore to a simmer, and put in the oven for 3 hours.

Brown the pork and sausage in a sauté pan, add to the pot, and return to the oven for ½ hour. Remove the pot from the oven. Arrange the sauerkraut over the meats and cover with the thinly sliced ham for a final ½ hour of cooking.

YIELD: 6–8 servings

RISOTTO WITH SAUSAGE

Of all the gifts of Italy, I am most grateful for risotto (aside from its sausages, of course). There are many shortcuts around for making risotto including baking and the use of microwave ovens. While these methods produce nice rice dishes, they don't produce risotto. Nothing compares with standing and stirring and a first-rate stock.

INGREDIENTS

- 5 cups (1.2 L) rich stock, either chicken or veal
- 3 tablespoons butter
- 2 teaspoons olive oil
- 2 tablespoons shallot, minced
- 2 cups (448 g) Arborio rice, no substitutes!
- ¾ pound (340 g) luganega sausage, cut into 2-inch (5 cm) pieces
- ¼ cup (60 mL) dry white wine
  Salt and pepper to taste
- 3 tablespoons Parmesan cheese, freshly grated
- 2 tablespoons water

METHOD

In a small pot bring the stock to a simmer. In a heavy pot, heat 2 tablespoons of the butter and the olive oil, add the shallot and cook until it is translucent. Add the rice and stir until each grain is coated in the oil and butter.

Add a ladleful of the hot stock to the rice, stirring constantly until the stock is visibly absorbed by the rice. As one ladle is absorbed add the next, stirring frequently. As the last of the stock is cooked into the rice, the rice starch and the stock will form a creamy sauce that will hold the dish together. The rice is done when it is no longer crunchy but only just chewy.

In the meantime, place the cut sausage and the wine in a skillet. Cook until the wine evaporates, then continue to cook the sausage in its fat until brown. When brown, remove the sausage and set aside. Keep the juices in the pan and set aside.

When the rice is risotto, mix in, very gently, the last tablespoon of butter and the Parmesan cheese. Mound the risotto on a platter, creating a hollow in the center of the mound.

Turn the heat on under the skillet containing the juice from the sausage. Pour off all but 1 tablespoon of fat and deglaze the pan with 2 tablespoons of water. Return the sausages to the pan and heat through.

To serve, place the sausages and their sauce in the hollow in the center of the risotto mound.

YIELD: 6 servings

SAUSAGE DUMPLINGS FOR SOUPS

These are useful to perk up a bland soup or to make it more filling. Since they are essentially little meatballs, they can be cooked as such. It is most efficient to make these with the forcemeat meat that's left over from stuffing normal links, then you can freeze them for future use.

INGREDIENTS

¼ cup (45 g) onion, minced

1 tablespoon butter

½ pound (224 g) sausage forcemeat

2 slices white bread, dipped in milk and mashed

2 egg yolks

¼ teaspoon nutmeg, grated

2 tablespoons Parmesan cheese, grated

1 quart (.95 L) chicken, beef, or vegetable stock

METHOD

Sauté the onion in butter until translucent. Cool slightly and mix with the sausage and all remaining ingredients, except for the stock. Mix thoroughly and form walnut-sized balls.

To cook, bring a quart of stock to a boil and drop in the dumplings. Reduce heat immediately to a simmer, and cook for 20 minutes. Add them either by themselves or with the broth, to a soup.

YIELD: Approximately 12 dumplings

CROSTINI WITH SAUSAGE AND CHEESE

These slices of toast, topped with the prepared sausage mixture, can serve as an hors d'oeuvre or as a luncheon dish.

INGREDIENTS

½ cup (224 g) ricotta cheese

3 tablespoons water (optional)

5 tablespoons Parmesan cheese, grated

½ teaspoon salt

3 links of Luganega or other mild garlic sausage

¼ cup (60 mL) water

¼ cup (56 g) butter

¼ cup (60 mL) olive oil

12 slices good white bread, you may remove the crusts

12 slices of Fontina or Gruyäre cheese, trimmed to fit the bread slices

METHOD

If the ricotta is dry, moisten it with the water, otherwise omit. Beat the Parmesan cheese and salt into the ricotta until creamy.

Preheat oven to 325°F (165°C). Cook sausages, using the poach and fry method—boil the sausages in a skillet with ¼ cup (60 mL) water until the water evaporates, then continue cooking until brown. Cool the sausage, chop fine, and mix into the cheese mixture.

In a clean skillet, heat the butter and olive oil and fry the bread until one side is golden brown. Spread a portion of the cheese mixture on the toasted side and place on a cookie sheet. Bake for 5 minutes, remove from the oven, and top each piece with a slice of cheese. Return the bread to the oven just long enough to melt the cheese.

YIELD: 12 servings

FAGIOLI DALL'OCCHIO CON SALSICCE
BLACK-EYED PEAS AND SAUSAGES IN TOMATO SAUCE

Combining these "beans with eyes" and garlic sausage creates a filling and tasty dish. The olive oil and tomatoes contribute to make this a sophisticated peasant stew.

INGREDIENTS

¼ cup (60 mL) olive oil

½ yellow onion, minced

1 clove fresh garlic, minced

½ cup (90 g) carrots, minced

½ cup (90 g) celery, minced

1 cup (224 g) canned tomatoes with their juice, roughly chopped

1 pound (448 g) Luganega (or other garlic sausage)

1 cup (224 g) dried black-eyed peas soaked in warm water for at least one hour

METHOD

Heat olive oil in the bottom of a heavy, ovenproof pot. Over medium heat, cook onions until translucent and yellowed from the olive oil. Add garlic until it colors slightly. Add carrots and celery and cook for five minutes, stirring occasionally. Finally, add tomatoes, turn heat to low, and simmer for 20 minutes.

Preheat oven to 350°F (150°C). Prick sausage four or five times each and add to pot, cooking slowly for 15 minutes. Drain the soaked peas and add to the pot. Add water to the stew, covering the ingredients by ½ inch (1.5 cm). Cover the pot, and bring to a simmer.

Place the covered pot in the oven and cook until peas are tender, approximately 1½ hours. Check occasionally and add water if necessary. If the peas are done and the stew is still soupy, return the pot to the top of the stove and cook over medium high heat until the liquid is reduced to a stew consistency. Before serving, tilt pot and ladle off excess fat.

YIELD: 4 servings

SAUSAGE EN CROUTE

Toad in the hole, pigs in a blanket, sausage rolls, party snacks; all taste even better with superior ingredients. The best sausage you can make of any size becomes transformed when wrapped attractively in almost any dough—short crust, puff pastry or brioche. Here is one possibility.

INGREDIENTS

      3 cups (420 g) flour
      1 teaspoon salt
3½ cups (840 mL) milk
      7 eggs
      ¾ cup (135 g) shallots, thinly sliced
      ½ cup (25 g) parsley, minced
      1 pound (448 g) sausage
      ¼ pound (112 g) slab bacon,
            cut into 1-inch (2.5 cm) pieces

METHOD

Preheat oven to 450˚F (230˚C). To make the batter, use an electric mixer on high speed to beat together all the ingredients, except the meats. (This is Yorkshire pudding, by the way.)

Fry the bacon with the sausage until the bacon is quite crisp but not burned. Pour all the fat into a meat loaf mold. Arrange the bacon and sausage evenly on the bottom of the mold. Pour the batter over it and bake for 10 minutes. Reduce the heat to 325˚F (165˚C), and bake 15 minutes longer. Slice and serve with the red pepper sauce.

YIELD: 6 servings

RED PEPPER SAUCE

Though this makes a perfect sauce for the en croute, you may use it whenever you need to add a little color and spice.

INGREDIENTS

      1 tablespoon butter
      ½ cup (90 g) onion, chopped
      3 red peppers, cored, seeded, and chopped
1¼ cups (300 mL) chicken stock
      ¼ cup (60 mL) white wine
            Salt and fresh-ground black pepper to taste

METHOD

Heat the butter in a saucepan over medium heat, and cook the onion until translucent. Add the red pepper and cook for 5 minutes, stirring frequently. Add the stock and wine, and simmer for 15 minutes.

Transfer the sauce to a blender and blend until completely smooth. Return to pan when ready to use, reheat and adjust for seasoning with salt and freshly ground black pepper.

YIELD: Approximately 2 cups (.6 L) of sauce

CLOCKWISE FROM TOP:
Horseradish sauce, Remoulade, and Mustard.

The sausage is grilled merguez served with pita bread and lemon wedges. (recipe on page 86)

sauces and condiments

Use the following recipes as complements to your prepared sausage when looking for compliments for your new sausage making skills. Invite friends over for a sausage tasting, lay out the condiments and accompaniments, chill the wine, frost the beer mugs, and have a celebration. Use the following sparingly or slather them on, but most of all enjoy them as the perfect grace notes to your great homemade sausages!

REMOULADE

This recipe is complex, although it is essentially a flavored mayonnaise. You can, if you like, substitute store-bought mayonnaise for the egg yolks and oil, and continue as below. Wait, on second thought, don't...it's better if you make your own. Trust me—a lot better!

INGREDIENTS

2 egg yolks

¼ cup (60 mL) vegetable oil

½ cup (90 g) celery, minced

½ cup (90 g) green onions, minced

¼ cup (12 g) fresh parsley, minced

¼ cup (90 g) fresh grated horseradish, or use ½ cup (180 g) prepared

¼ lemon, seeds removed then finely chopped—rind included

1 bay leaf

2 tablespoons Creole mustard (I like Zaterain's)

2 tablespoons catsup

1 tablespoon hot mustard

1 tablespoon white vinegar

1 tablespoon tabasco sauce

1 tablespoon fresh garlic, minced

2 teaspoons paprika

1 teaspoon salt

METHOD

Use a blender or food processor. First add the eggs yolks and beat for approximately 2 minutes until they are thick and pale yellow.

With the machine running, add the oil in a thin stream. (Voila, you have made mayonnaise—wasn't that easy?). Add each successive ingredient, one at a time, until well blended. Remember to use the entire lemon piece, being certain that it and its rind is finely chopped before placing in the machine.

YIELD: Approximately 2 cups (.55 L)

MUSTARD

If ever wars have been fought over sausages, battles also have been waged over mustard. I cannot claim to present the definitive recipe—nor am I divulging any family secrets. This mustard delivers a sweet-sour, spicy tang with just a faint hint of brewed hops and barley.

INGREDIENTS

6 tablespoons mustard seeds

½ cup (56 g) dry mustard

¼ cup (60 mL) cider vinegar

¼ cup (40 g) brown sugar

1 teaspoon salt

2 cloves fresh garlic, minced

¼ teaspoon allspice

¼ teaspoon cloves

¼ teaspoon fresh tarragon

1 tablespoon honey

¾ cup (180 mL) pale, dry beer

METHOD

Using a blender or food processor, place the mustard seeds and dry mustard in the machine. Place the other ingredients, except for the honey and beer, in a saucepan. Bring to a boil, then pour into the machine with the dry mustard and seeds. Process until smooth.

Leave the mixture in your machine for three hours, add the honey and beer, and reprocess. Keep refrigerated in a tightly closed jar for several months.

YIELD: 2 cups (.55 L)

SALSA VERDE

This sauce is excellent with all poached sausages, hot or cold. It is equally good served with all cold meats as well as with fish dishes.

INGREDIENTS

4 anchovies, mashed, or 1 tablespoon of anchovy paste

1 medium potato, boiled and mashed

2 tablespoons onion, finely minced

1 clove fresh garlic, minced

½ cup (25 g) parsley, chopped

6 small sour gherkins, minced, preferably French cornichon or Italian cetriolini sott'aceto

6 tablespoons olive oil

2 tablespoons lemon juice

2 tablespoons white wine vinegar

METHOD

I find it is easiest to mix the ingredients in a jar that holds more than a pint (480 mL) and has a tight-fitting lid. As you add each ingredient, shake thoroughly.

Otherwise, assemble the ingredients, and in a stainless steel bowl, whisk everything but the olive oil, lemon juice, and vinegar. When the ingredients are combined, add, 1 tablespoon at a time, all of the olive oil, shaking or beating after each addition. Finally, stir in the lemon juice and vinegar.

YIELD: Approximately 2 cups (.55 mL)

HORSERADISH SAUCE

This sauce is excellent to serve with any boiled meat and many vegetable dishes. Dip browned sausage "coins" pierced with cocktail picks into this or any of the previous sauces at a buffet or pass them around at a party.

INGREDIENTS

2 tablespoons butter

1½ tablespoons flour

1 cup (240 mL) milk

3 tablespoons prepared horseradish, or 1½ tablespoons fresh grated

2 tablespoons whipping cream

1 teaspoon sugar

1 teaspoon dry mustard

1 tablespoon vinegar

METHOD

This is best served right after making it. First, make a white roux. Heat the butter over a low heat, then, using a wire whisk, gradually add the flour. Cook for 3 to 4 minutes to cook off the raw flavor of flour. Very gradually, stir in the milk until thoroughly blended and the sauce begins to thicken. Remove from the heat and add remaining ingredients. Reheat without boiling, and serve.

YIELD: Approximately 1½ cups (360 mL)

PEPPERS IN OLIVE OIL

Easy to make and wonderful to eat, serve these peppers with grilled sausages, particularly salsiccie or luganega. Add a few hot peppers and serve with spicy chorizo or merguez. For a classic sandwich, start with grilled sausage and crusty bread. Lay the peppers and oil on top, allowing the flavored olive oil to soak into the bread.

INGREDIENTS

3 bell peppers, for added color use one each of green, red, and yellow

Olive oil

Oregano, dried

Salt to taste

METHOD

Cut the peppers in half lengthwise, removing the cores and seeds. Cut the peppers into strips and place in a pot. Add olive oil to half the depth of the peppers. Add approximately 3 tablespoons (more if desired) of dried oregano, and stir. Place over medium high heat. Get the oil hot but not boiling. At this point, reduce the heat to low and cover. Allow the peppers to stew until soft. As they cook, occasionally shake the pot with the cover on to blend the oil and herb through the peppers. Salt to taste. Serve immediately or keep in the refrigerator for five days. Reheat to serve.

YIELD: 4–6 servings

what to drink?

According to an informal online survey by the National Hot Dog and Sausage Council, most people prefer Italian sausage and Polish kielbasa. Their number one beverage of choice to accompany them? Beer.

glossary

BULK SAUSAGE Forcemeat that is not stuffed into a casing but usually formed into patties before cooking. It may also be cooked until it crumbles before being added to recipes.

CASING Any wrapper that surrounds the forcemeat. Most commonly a pork, beef, or sheep intestine, it can also be a vegetable leaf, paper, or a muslin bag.

CURING A method of preserving meat by removing most of the moisture. Chemical curing agents, most commonly nitrates and nitrites, are added to prevent the meat from spoiling as it dries.

DEGLAZE The use of liquid to lift any residue remaining in a pan from the frying process (the bits that are "glazed" to the pan) for the purpose of making a sauce or gravy.

EMULSIFY To grind meat into a very fine, paste-like mixture for the purpose of evenly distributing the fat.

FORCEMEAT The ground or emulsified meat that has been mixed with other ingredients such as herbs, spices, and vegetables.

NATURAL CASING Casings made from the submucosa, which is a largely collagen layer of the intestine.

PACKING To stuff a sausage casing with forcemeat.

PAR FREEZE Partially frozen.

POACHING To cook or semi-cook in water that is near the boiling point for a short amount of time.

SAUSAGE Finely chopped and seasoned meat that is usually stuffed into a casing before being cooked or cured.

SMOKING Using a smoky fire to impart flavor to, or to preserve meat. Cold smoking imparts flavor but does not cook the meat. Hot smoking imparts flavor and cooks the meat.

bibliography

Aidells, Bruce and Dennis Kelly. *Flying Sausages.* San Francisco: Chronicle Books, 1995.

Armstrong, Alison. *The Joyce of Cooking: Food and Drink from James Joyce's Dublin.* Barrytown, NY: Station Hill Press, 1986.

Child, Julia. *The French Chef Cookbook.* New York: Alfred A. Knopf, 1968.

Glen, Camille. *The Heritage of Southern Cooking.* New York: Workman Publishing, 1986.

Hazan, Marcella. *The Classic Italian Cook Book.* New York: Harper's Magazine Press, 1973.

Hippsley Coxe, Antony and Araminta Hippsley Coxe. *The Great Book of Sausages.* Woodstock, NY: The Overlook Press, 1996.

Kennedy, Diana. *The Cuisines of Mexico.* New York: Harper and Rowe, 1972.

Kuo, Irene. *The Key to Chinese Cooking.* New York: Alfred A. Knopf, 1981.

Kutas, Rytek. *Great Sausage Recipes and Meat Curing.* Buffalo, NY: MacMillan, 1987.

Lobel, Leon and Stanley Lobel. *All About Meat.* New York: Harcourt Brace Jovanovitch, 1975.

Merinoff, Linda. *The Savory Sausage: A Culinary Tour Around the World.* New York: Poseidon Press, Simon and Schuster, Inc., 1987.

Montagné, Prosper. *Larousse Gastronomique The Encyclopedia of Food, Wine, and Cookery.* 1st American ed. New York: Crown Publishers, Inc., 1961.

Neal, Bill. *Biscuits, Spoon Bread, and Sweet Potato Pie.* New York: Alfred A. Knopf, 1990.

Prudhomme, Paul. *Chef Paul Prudhomme's Louisiana Kitchen.* New York: William Morrow, 1984.

Reavis, Charles G. *Home Sausage Making.* Rev. ed. Pownal, VT: Garden Way Publishing, Storey Communications, Inc., 1987.

Thorne, John. *Simple Cooking.* New York: Viking, 1987.

metric equivalents

SOLID MEASUREMENT
in grams (g) and kilograms (kg)

U.S.	Metric
¼ pound	112 g
⅓ pound	148 g
½ pound	224 g
⅔ pound	297 g
¾ pound	336 g
1 pound	448 g
1¼ pounds	560 g
1½ pounds	672 g
2 pounds	896 g
2¼ pounds	1 kg
2½ pounds	1.1 kg
3 pounds	1.4 kg
3½ pounds	1.6 kg
4 pounds	1.8 kg
4½ pounds	2 kg
5 pounds	2.2 kg

FLUID MEASUREMENT
in milliliters (mL) and liters (L)

U.S.	Metric
1 teaspoon	5 mL
1 tablespoon (3 teaspoons)	15 mL
2 tablespoons (1 ounce)	30 mL
¼ cup	60 mL
⅓ cup	90 mL
½ cup	120 mL
¾ cup	180 mL
1 cup	240 mL
2 cups	.47 L
1 quart	.95 L
1½ quart	1.4 L
2 quarts	1.9 L

¼ cup = 2 fluid ounces
½ cup = 4 fluid ounces)
1 cup = 8 fluid ounces
2 cups = 1 pint
2 pints = 1 quart

LENGTH

U.S.	Metric
1 inch	2.5 cm

TEMPERATURE EQUIVALENTS

170°F = 78°C
180°F = 82°C
190°F = 88°C
200°–205°F = 95°C
220°–225°F = 120°C
245°–250°F = 120°C
275°F = 135°C
300°–305°F = 150°C
325°–330°F = 165°C
345°–350°F = 175°C
370°–375°F = 190°C
400°–405°F = 205°C
425°–430°F = 220°C
445°–450°F = 230°C
470°–475°F = 245°C
500°F = 260°C

TO CONVERT FAHRENHEIT TO CELSIUS:
subtract 32, multiply by 5, and divide by 9

OVEN TEMPERATURES

U.S.	Metric
32°F (water freezes)	0°C
212°F	100°C
300°F (slow oven)	150°C
350°F (moderate oven)	175°C
400°F (hot oven)	205°C

sausage-makers'
sources for Equipment, Supplies, and Information

ALLIED KENCO SALES

26 Lyerly St.
Houston, TX 77022

PHONE: 713-691-2935

TOLL FREE: 800-356-5189

FAX: 713-691-3250

E-MAIL: aks@alliedkenco.com

"Everything but the meat"
*Equipment, casings, spices,
seasoning kits, starter kits*

MICHLITCH CO., INC.

210 W. Pacific Avenue
Spokane, WA 99201-0124

PHONE: 509-624-1490

FAX: 509-624-0822

WEBSITE: www.mitlitch.com

*Equipment, casings, spices,
books*

NETO SASAUGE CO.

3499 The Alameda
Santa Clara, CA 95050

MAILING ADDRESS:
PO Box 578
Santa Clara, CA 95052

PHONE: 408-296-0818

TOLL FREE: 888-482-NETO (6386)

FAX: 408-296-0538

WEB SITE: www.netosausage.com

Sheep casings

STUFFERS SUPPLY COMPANY

2298 Fraser Highway
Langly BC V2Z 2T9
Canada

PHONE: 604-534-7374

FAX: 604-534-3089

Equipment, casings, seasonings

index